T0167968

PENGUIN
SPECIALS

Penguin Specials fill a gap. Written by some of today's most exciting and insightful writers, they are short enough to be read in a single sitting – when you're stuck on a train; in your lunch hour; between dinner and bedtime. Specials can provide a thought-provoking opinion, a primer to bring you up to date, or a striking piece of fiction. They are concise, original and affordable.

To browse digital and print Penguin Specials titles, please refer to **www.penguin.com.au/penguinspecials**

ALSO BY PAUL FRENCH

Bloody Saturday

Shanghai's Darkest Day

PAUL FRENCH

PENGUIN BOOKS

UK | USA | Canada | Ireland | Australia
India | New Zealand | South Africa | China

Penguin Books is part of the Penguin Random House group of companies
whose addresses can be found at global.penguinrandomhouse.com.

First published by Penguin Group (Australia) in association
with Penguin (Beijing) Ltd, 2017

1 3 5 7 9 10 8 6 4 2

Cover design by Di Suo © Penguin Group (Australia)
Cover photograph © Virtual Shanghai (Institut d'Asie Orientale)
Text design by Steffan Leyshon-Jones © Penguin Group (Australia)
Printed and bound in Hong Kong by Printing Express

penguin.com.au

ISBN: 9780734398550

A NOTE ON SPELLING

Throughout this book I have used the Wade-Giles romanisations of Chinese provinces, districts, rivers, creeks, towns and cities, as these would have been in common use in 1937. The current pinyin romanisations are listed in the appendix of this book for clarification.

Prologue: The Approaching Storm

A Shanghai August is invariably a hot and humid affair. The city's population swelters in the airless heat that begins each daybreak, giving little respite until the few cool hours before dawn of the following day. Residents able to afford electricity in 1937 ran their desktop Swan fans all night long, and nightclubs that advertised air conditioning consequently attracted good business. Other venues simply placed large blocks of melting ice in the middle of the dancefloor to keep the temperature down. The Shanghainese dragged camp beds into the *lilong* alleyways and slept outside to avoid the stifling indoor conditions.

What traditionally offers Shanghai some relief in August are the rains and gusts of wind swept towards the city from the edges of the typhoons that rage out in the South China Sea. It is one of Shanghai's secrets of success that the city is, normally, typhoon-free. They sweep across the sea, causing annual devastation in Taiwan and the Philippines. If typhoons make land-fall on China's coast it is usually further to the south, below Amoy, down to Hong Kong and Macao.

Some erroneous weather reports stated that Shanghai was hit by a typhoon of 'violent intensity' that August. But what really struck the city was a man-made assault of bombs, shrapnel and bullets, bringing aerial death and destruction such as no city had ever seen before.

Throughout the 1930s, governments had greatly feared the devastation aerial bombing could cause in the event of war. From the very inception of planes, their military importance had been recognised – not least in H.G. Wells' 1907 science-fiction novel *The War in the Air*. The German Zeppelin raids on London and other English towns in the First World War had been a portent of what might come.

Certainly, Prime Minister Stanley Baldwin summed up the general fear of aerial bombing and the destruc-tion it might cause when he told the British parliament in 1932, 'I think it is well also for the man in the street to realise that there is no power on earth that can protect him from being bombed. Whatever people may tell him, the bomber will always get through.'

Certainly Baldwin's analysis seemed to have been

borne out in April 1937 when the German Condor Legion bombed the Spanish town of Guernica. That horrific aerial onslaught prompted Picasso's mural-sized oil painting. Completed that June, *Guernica* detailed the horror of the devastation, and elicited both outrage at the fascist bombers and sympathy for the Spanish Republican cause when it was exhibited at the Paris Exposition.

The bombs that fell on Shanghai just several months after Guernica, on 14 August 1937, also fell on unprepared civilians, but in the world's fifth largest, and by far most densely populated, city of three and a half million people.

Over one thousand civilians were killed at Guernica; at Shanghai, over two thousand lives were lost and many more were injured. 'Bloody Saturday', as it quickly became known, was a portent of what was to come to other cities including Chungking, London, Manchester, Liverpool, Antwerp, Berlin, Dresden, Tokyo, and so many others in the Second World War.

The Last Moments Before War

That August, a typhoon raged unexpectedly close to the coast and prevented commercial shipping from entering the port of Shanghai. Heavy gales blew in from the sea, toppling trees, bringing down telegraph poles and causing havoc for the city's telephone system. Scheduled steamer departures were delayed and commercial air services between Shanghai and Canton were temporarily suspended. Only the hardiest of rickshaw pullers remained on the streets.

The Whangpoo River that runs through the centre of Shanghai, with the densely populated International Settlement to the west and the industrial and agricultural Pootung district to the east, was free of the clutter of steamers, lighters, liners and tramps that usually swarmed the waterway. Dominating the Whangpoo, adjacent to Shanghai's majestic Bund waterfront, were the battleships of several nations in what was known as 'Battleship Alley'.

As the storm skirted Shanghai traffic and pedestrians appeared once more on the streets, ships finally departed port while others docked and air services partially resumed. Life in the International Settlement of Shanghai, run by a foreign-dominated Municipal Council, equipped with its own police force and courts, returned to normal. The neighbouring French Concession, also known as Frenchtown, similarly picked itself up and resumed business. However, across Soochow Creek in the north, things were about to become far less placid. Here were the sprawling Hongkew and Yangtzepoo districts, as well as the Chinese-controlled portions of the city comprising Chapei, Paoshan and Kiangwan.

Texan Claire Lee Chennault had retired after twenty years of service from the American Army Air Corps on 30 April 1937; the next day he boarded a ship for China. He had been appointed to a three-month contract to produce a confidential survey of the Chinese Air Force (CAF) for the Nanking government.

Chennault was aware of American involvement in China's fledgeling CAF. Americans had established the Central Aviation School at Hangchow.

Chennault, who looked more like a prize-fighter than one of America's top military strategists, arrived in June after a stop in Japan to snoop around the country's air defence and attack capabilities. He sat down to tea with his new boss, Soong May-ling, better known as Madame Chiang, the powerful wife of China's Generalissimo Chiang Kai-shek. Convinced that Nationalist China needed a modern air force, it had been May-ling

Claire Lee Chennault

who had pushed for its development and championed the CAF cause.

During Chennault's stay in Nanking, the Japanese had invaded Peking and he found himself suddenly promoted from an outside observer to a key strategist in the planning of Nationalist China's response to the onslaught. At the time, Chennault had noted in his diary that 'the Chinese Air Force is not ready for war.'

Peking and Tientsin had fallen to Japanese invasion in mid-July. While battles raged across the broad swathe of Northern China from Jehol to Mongolia, Shanghai remained calm on China's eastern seaboard. Rumours ran rife that Chiang Kai-shek and his Nationalist government had done a deal with Tokyo – the Japanese could control China north of the Yangtze if he was left to run the country to the south of the river. Many believed it, though it wasn't true. Japan's aggression was not to be appeased.

*

On Monday, 9 August, two Japanese soldiers tried to force their way into Shanghai's Hungjao Aerodrome to the west of the city. They were shot by Chinese Peace Preservation Corps guards, armed *gendarmes* and the only Chinese force in the area, one of whom was killed in the attack. The Japanese press dubbed the incident

'The Aerodrome Murders', inciting Japanese public opinion against China.

The Chinese said it was a provocation by the Japanese; Tokyo said the incident was staged by the Chinese to excuse the movement of troops into Shanghai. Either way, Japan ordered its warships to converge on Shanghai; in response China moved the elite Eighty-Eighth Division closer to the city.

On Wednesday 11 August, the Japanese Third Fleet arrived. The flagship armoured cruiser *Idzumo* was accompanied by an aircraft carrier, the *Kaga*, and fourteen other naval craft. They anchored in the Whangpoo River, directly in front of the International Settlement. The *Idzumo* remained just offshore from the Japanese Consulate.

American journalist Vanya Oakes had pitched up in

Battle Cruiser *Idzumo* moored alongside the Japanese Consulate

Vanya Oakes

Shanghai in 1933 thinking to escape the Depression back home and find a job. She did, at the *China Press* newspaper, an American-run English language daily. Oakes was between apartments and staying at the Astor House Hotel in Hongkew, just over the Soochow Creek, opposite the Soviet Consulate and a stone's throw from the heavily sandbagged and protected Japanese Consulate. That night she lay in bed and nervously listened to the hum of the *Idzumo's* generators close by on the Whangpoo.

Further troop transports loaded with Japanese Marines anchored downriver. Over five thousand Marines of the Japanese Special Naval Landing Forces went ashore at the privately-owned wharves of the Osaka Shosen Kaisha, Nippon Yusen Kaisha and the Mitsui Bussan Kaisha corporations, as well as the Japanese

Naval jetties, all on the Pootung side of the Whangpoo opposite the Yangtzepoo and Hongkew districts of the International Settlement. The Japanese Naval Command demanded that all Chinese troops retreat to a distance of thirty miles or more from Shanghai. The Chinese refused and ordered up the modernised and well-trained Eighty-Seventh Division from Nanking to join the Eighty-Eighth, the two best-trained Divisions of the newly formed Ninth Army Group.

At dawn on Thursday 12 August, the Japanese gunboats *Seta* and *Kuri* began to shell the Chinese portions of northern Shanghai from their anchorages on the Whangpoo. Outside the International Settlement's borders, the Chinese-administered districts of Chapei and Kiangwan took the brunt of the shelling. Most cannon fire was aimed towards the buildings of Shanghai University where, close by, the Japanese landing forces intended to build an airfield to allow them to ferry in additional men and material to the city.

Australian Rhodes Farmer was the roving war correspondent for the *Melbourne Herald*. He had been in China for less than a year, '. . . learning the ins and outs of chopsticks and Far Eastern politics (which mostly go together) in Shanghai.' Farmer watched the Japanese begin to fortify their positions around Chapei and witnessed the start of the shelling.

One evening the Chinese suburb seemed normal enough, its alleyways crowded with gossiping merchants and shop owners smoking their long pipes in the cool of the evening, and children playing their eternal Chinese version of hopscotch. But by dawn thousands of Chinese soldiers had moved in, silent as nighthawks on straw sandals . . .

The naval bombardment of Chapei was followed by incursions from Japanese troops in Midget two-man tanks and foot patrols. The Japanese brought up field guns to support the fighting along the Shanghai-Woosung rail line. A total of thirty-three Japanese battleships were now gathered at Shanghai, or close by at Woosung, and so control of the rail line was crucial for the Japanese if they were to speedily reinforce their troops in the city.

The fighting was fiercest around Hongkew Park and the rifle range where the Japanese command were bunkering in. *United Press* correspondent H.R. 'Bud' Ekins drove up to the park with his colleague John Morris, another veteran reporter who had been based in Nanking and was friendly with Madame Chiang.

Ekins and Morris saw Japanese motorcycles with machine guns mounted on the pillions and a Midget tank guarding the crossing of the Shanghai-Woosung rail line. Moving between Hongkew Park and the North

Railway Station they encountered erratic sniper fire. The Chinese Army were erecting concrete pillboxes, sandbagging street corners and digging tank traps. During the day the North Railway Station's sturdy ferroconcrete administrative building was turned into a fortress. From the roof, spotters could see the Japanese Special Naval Landing troops in Hongkew. Meanwhile Chinese Peace Preservation Forces, local militarised police units, were mobilised and began patrols of the Soochow Creek's embankments and the Chinese-controlled portions of Chapei. They rolled out barbed wire and re-fortified all strategic street corners close to the North Railway Station, pointed their guns eastwards and waited.

The area around the station was contested territory with checkpoints established by both the Japanese Army and the Russian detachment of the local territorials, the Shanghai Volunteer Corps (SVC). Close by, on Range Road, a Japanese post was under constant fire from Chinese snipers positioned in nearby houses and on rooftops. John Morris was forced to find sanctuary in a Buddhist temple on Range Road, within the Japanese-controlled zone. He borrowed their telephone to call in his on-the-spot observations to the *United Press* offices over the other side of Soochow Creek on the Avenue Edward VII. It was crowded and noisy – three hundred Japanese refugees from nearby 'Little Tokyo' were seeking sanctuary on straw mats in the temple.

Madame Chiang had asked Claire Lee Chennault to fly to Shanghai and report back to her on the situation. Chennault observed the build-up of Japanese troops north of Soochow Creek and witnessed the arrival of the Japanese Third Fleet. He returned to Nanking on the afternoon of Friday 13 to sit in on the Generalissimo's War Council. Chiang informed the Council on what Chennault had seen with his own eyes, that the *Idzumo* and other Japanese ships had started to shell Chapei, and that they were the major support for the Japanese land forces. Madame Chiang asked Chennault to recommend action in retaliation. He advocated sending bombers to attack the *Idzumo*. As there were no Chinese air officers experienced in this sort of operation, Chennault was asked to take charge. The Chinese presented an ultimatum to the Japanese demanding they withdraw their troops from Chapei by 4 p.m., or face retaliation.

The International Settlement moved to protect itself as the Chinese quarters in the north of the city burned. Admiral Harry F. Yarnell, the commander of America's thirty-nine vessel-strong Asiatic Fleet in the Far East, was aboard his flagship USS *Augusta* moored offshore from Tsingtao. Yarnell gave the order to weigh anchor and steam the three hundred and sixty-seven nautical miles southwards at full speed to Shanghai to take charge of American forces in the city. He cabled ahead orders for troops aboard the *USS Sacramento*, already stationed in the Whangpoo's Battleship Alley, to immediately go ashore and take up guard positions in the Yangtzepoo district, close to the bombed Chinese areas. They built sandbagged machinegun emplacements outside the generators of the Shanghai Power Company to prevent the city being plunged into total darkness. Further American Navy guards were placed outside the Socony-Vacuum oil terminal and Texaco's Shanghai terminal.

Likewise, the British North Lancashire Regiment, known as the 'Loyals', stationed in the Settlement, mustered for action. Britain had a total of nine hundred and fifty soldiers in the city. They prepared sandbags and machine gun emplacements along the southern banks of Soochow Creek, typically filled with sampans, and stood ready to repel any Japanese advance southwards, down from Chapei and into the central Settlement. Soldiers began running field telephone lines along Brenan Road, on the far western borders of the Settlement by Jessfield Park, to ensure continued communication if the city's telephone system went down. Rhodes Farmer began to report from the British side of the barbed wire perimeter where the Lancashire Loyals were embedded.

The American and British consulates used local radio station X.H.M.A. and the late editions of the *Shanghai*

Evening Post to advise all their nationals to evacuate the Chinese portions of northern Shanghai to the southern side of Soochow Creek. The idea was to move them to safety, but it was still a dangerous operation that exposed civilians to trigger-happy Japanese soldiers who were roaming the streets. One British man was shot dead crossing the creek as well as three White Russian refugees who were attempting to flee across from the Chapei side. Standing guard near the contested North Railway Station, a British SVC member was shot and wounded in the shoulder.

John Morris left his Buddhist temple phone booth to drive back to the relative safety of the International Settlement south of Soochow Creek. Heading down through Chapei, Morris was surprised to see a lone foreigner walking south and stopped to offer him a lift – Max Hirsch, a German and a long-time resident of Chapei's Scott Road. Herr Hirsch was 'nonchalantly' strolling towards the Settlement border with his three dachshunds.

John Morris dropped Hirsch and his dachshunds off and parked up by the Broadway Mansions, a magnificent art-deco apartment building adjacent to the Garden Bridge, right on the northern bank of Soochow Creek at the junction with the Whangpoo and facing the Bund across. It was home to many foreign journalists. Randall Gould, a former *United Press* colleague, ran an office largely out of his apartment in the building. Gould, a tall Minnesotan, had worked in Japan before moving to China in the 1920s to work for the newspaper. He reputedly knew every correspondent, stringer and hack writer in the Far East and had a network second to none that extended from Honolulu to Yokohama, Manila to Hong Kong, and all points in between. Gould was now the China correspondent for the *Christian Science Monitor* and the editor of the *Shanghai Evening Post & Mercury*.

Morris joined Gould on the roof of the nineteen-storey building to watch the Japanese shelling of Chapei and the North Railway Station. They saw three shells fired and fall from the *Idzumo*, a brief pause for the artillery observers to calibrate the range, and then another volley of shells. The two men watched the Japanese repeat the operation again, and again, and again . . .

Colonel Charles F.B. Price was a China veteran. He had been the Officer-in-Charge at the American Legation in Peking in the 1920s and was now the commanding officer of the one thousand United States Fourth Marines in Shanghai. With the commencement of the Japanese shelling of Chapei, Price recalled his men to the barracks and ordered them to prepare for 'any eventuality'.

The foreign-manned SVC was summoned on Friday night to protect the forty-nine thousand foreigners

Commander Charles FB Price

resident in the Settlement. The SVC was divided into companies along national and specialist lines. All members were volunteers recalled from their day jobs at times of emergency and were spread out across the Settlement. One and a half thousand SVC members were present in the city to muster themselves immediately. The Shanghai Scottish and Jewish companies were billeted in the Rowing Club adjacent to Soochow Creek, just across the road from the sprawling British Consulate's compound. The SVC's Air Defence detachment was stationed close by in the gardens of the Union Church.

'B' Battalion, composed of the American, Portuguese, Philippines and American Machine Gun companies, had occupied the Polytechnic Public School on Pakhoi Road, close to the Shanghai Racecourse, while 'C' Battalion, predominantly manned by White Russian refugees to Shanghai and the only full-time company in the corps, occupied a number of block houses on Elgin Road on the far side of Soochow Creek, close to the North Railway Station. The Russians had immediately begun helping the Chinese Army defend the station to fill canvas bags with sand to barricade their position. A Chinese detachment of the SVC, along with a group of interpreters who aided communication between the linguistically myriad companies, was stationed in the Cathedral Boy's School in the cloisters of the Shanghai Cathedral on Kiukiang Road. Despite the hostilities with the Japanese Army, the Japanese Company of the Corps had still been mobilised and stationed only two streets away from the North Railway Station on Boone Road.

White Russian refugee Boris Ivanovich was watching a movie that evening at the Metropole Cinema on Thibet Road in the French Concession. Halfway through the night's main feature – *Hollywood Cowboy*, a Wild West adventure with George O'Brien – a slide flashed on the screen ordering all members of the SVC to immediately report to their companies for mobilisation orders. Boris felt a chill run down his spine. He was just seventeen years old and had lied about his age to get into the corps. He was one of the newest recruits and still hadn't been issued with an official uniform. As Ivanovich and the other SVC members in the stalls stood up to leave the cinema, the audience applauded them. Ivanovich's muster point was close by at the Avenue Joffre Fire Station. He walked the few blocks east along the wide street and reported for duty. He was assigned a bunk for the night and told to await orders.

The authorities in the French Concession announced a general curfew that would go into operation between the hours of 10 p.m. and 5 a.m. from Sunday 15 August until the emergency in Chapei was over. The Shanghai Municipal Council followed suit several hours later, announcing their own curfew regulations to go into effect the following week.

Nicolai Alexandrovich Slobodchikoff was, like young Boris Ivanovich, a White Russian. His family had been one of the many hundreds of thousands who could find no accommodation with the Bolsheviks after the 1917 October Revolution and left the country, becoming stateless émigrés. The Slobodchikoffs had headed east, across Siberia and eventually into China. They had settled in Shanghai along with thousands of other refugee White families. Nicolai had studied mechanical engineering in Belgium, but when he returned to Shanghai, he couldn't find a job to match his education. Like so many Russians of the middle and upper classes, he spoke fluent French and so joined the French Concession's police force, the *Garde Municipal*. On the evening of Friday the thirteenth, all leave was cancelled and Slobodchikoff reported for duty at

No.22 Route Stanislas Chevalier, French Police HQ.

Leave was also cancelled for members of Shanghai's Municipal Fire Service. R. Somers was the Assistant Station Officer at the Shanghai Central Fire Station on Foochow Road, a few blocks from the Cathay Hotel. Close to the offices of the Municipal Council and the headquarters of the Shanghai Municipal Police, the four storey Central Fire Station was crowned with the motto 'We Fight the Flames' in Ningbo-glazed green tiles over the red brick frontage. Somers reported for duty, dragged out a camp bed and tried to get some sleep.

That evening the Japanese cabinet in Tokyo announced on the radio that they would order 'concrete measures' to be taken to destroy Chinese resistance in Shanghai. Premier Prince Fumimaro Konoye stated that he would broadcast to the nation on Sunday. The title of his address would be 'The Determination of the Imperial Navy'. Japanese newspapers reported that voluntary contributions to the nation's war chest from across Japan had exceeded US$2.5 million.

A refugee crisis immediately emerged as terrified and bombed out Chinese from Chapei and Kiangwan attempted to reach the safety of the Settlement. An outbreak of sniping across the North Szechuen Road between Chinese and Japanese soldiers sent civilians scuttling for cover on the busy commercial street. Rents for available rooms in the Settlement and Frenchtown immediately soared – a room that rented for eight Chinese dollars a week on Thursday 12 August rented for twenty-five and upwards the next day. The Shanghai Municipal Police remained on duty at their most northerly station on Hongkew's Dixwell Road and attempted to locate the legion of fires that had broken out and were left untreated across the northern districts. Fire engines heading towards Chapei from the Settlement were jeered, stoned and barricaded from getting through by the Japanese residents of Hongkew's Little Tokyo.

On Friday 13, ships took advantage of the eye of the storm to leave port. An exodus of nervous Shanghai-landers, foreign residents of the city, began to board evacuating ships where they were able to. The Japanese passenger steamers *Shanghai Maru* and *Nagasaki Maru* sailed in the morning, full to capacity, including many Americans who had decided to head home. The ships, headed for Kobe and on to America's West Coast, were delayed at the mouth of the Whangpoo by the final effects of the typhoon and Japanese Imperial Navy ships claiming concern for passenger safety.

At noon, all Chinese banks were closed; foreign banks remained open for the time being but convened an emergency meeting to consider a restriction of withdrawals to prevent a panicked run on the city's money supply.

Firemen try to extinguish a fire in Chapei

The Chinese feared a Japanese naval attack on the aerodrome at Lunghwa. After the liners departed, a line of scuttled ships was sunk across the Whangpoo above the Quai de France (the French Bund), adjacent to Shanghai's Nantao old town, to prevent any more departures. A further ten steamers, including several confiscated by the Chinese from Japanese shipping lines, were partially submerged, just south of Kiangyin on the Yangtze in Kiangsu Province, blocking river communication between Shanghai, China's most important commercial city, and Nanking, the nation's embattled capital.

Saturday 14 August, 1937

The early morning sky was overcast. The typhoon had not yet passed completely and intermittent rainstorms still blew in from Shanghai along the Yangtze River. Heavy winds and rain lashed the city periodically.

Vanya Oakes hadn't moved from her lodgings at the Astor House Hotel. For two days she had been out reporting on the advance of Japanese troops across Hongkew and their assault on Chapei. On Friday evening, exhausted and after a long hot bath, she had come down to dinner in the hotel's famous Grill Room. Several Japanese families had come in to dine but the Chinese staff refused to serve them. The Grill Room's Swiss *maître d'hôtel* ordered the staff to serve the Japanese families. The Chinese staff refused and the *maître d'* was forced to serve them himself.

Colleagues urged Vanya to move into another hotel in the central part of the Settlement, indeed the management of the Astor themselves were advising people to move out of the precariously placed institution. Oakes planned to report on the fighting in Chapei the next day and decided to stay put. At dawn on Saturday morning, she walked out of the Astor into the streets of Hongkew towards Chapei. She saw,

> . . . silhouettes loom out of the darkness, gaunt, grim. Bayonets and helmets – moving. The clank of heavy machinery, the groan of wheels, muffled, ominous, indeterminate sounds. Lying close to the wharves the superstructures of ships showed skeletonized, the noses of guns glowering up into the sky. Thump-clump – thump-clump – thump-clu-u-u-u . . .

The typhoon left a blanket of dark cloud over the Settlement. In his office at Broadway Mansions, Randall Gould had started monitoring the renewed shelling of Chapei at 7 a.m. from his rooftop eyrie and was still there several hours later. John Morris stopped by to see him again but had to leave for a working lunch at the Cathay Hotel with his reporting partner Bud Ekins. Gould stayed behind to keep watch and report on the action. As Morris was leaving, the *Idzumo*'s massive guns once again opened fire towards Chapei, creating enormous crescendos that rattled his teeth. He encountered Judge Milton Helmick of the US Court for China in Shanghai who was sheltering in the lobby from the bombardment. The two men acknowledged each other (Morris was actually dating the Judge's niece at the time) and tried to act as if it were just another Shanghai Saturday morning.

Claire Lee Chennault's plan was to send a squadron of American-made Curtiss Model 68 Hawk III dive-bombers against the Japanese cruisers massed on the Whangpoo, followed by a squadron of CAF Northrop light bombers to target the *Idzumo* flagship. The Curtiss Hawk was the CAF's frontline fighter, but could also be used as a dive-bomber with a top speed of over two hundred miles per hour.

Chennault was aware that a Japanese response would come quickly – first in the form of anti-aircraft fire from the *Idzumo* and ground positions, and then from fighter planes catapulted from the deck of the aircraft carrier *Kaga*. Chinese aircrews had been trained at Hangchow to fly at seven and a half thousand feet at a set speed. This was clearly too high to preclude the possibility of missing the targets in such a confined area, and risked hitting the crowded International Settlement or Pootung on the far side of the river. The need for accuracy, coupled with the low cloud that day, meant the pilots had to fly at just one and a half thousand feet, a low altitude the pilots had not been adequately trained for. Flying at this level over such a densely populated city was a recipe for disaster even for a highly trained bomb sighter. The crews were ordered to stand ready while Chennault considered his options.

Vanya Oakes may have decided to stay in Hongkew, but others had heeded the advice of their consulates to relocate. Japanese-born Dr Robert Reischauer was a professor of international relations at Princeton. The son of American missionaries in Tokyo, Reischauer was leading a Far East study tour with ten American political scientists. Reischauer and his party had been staying at the Astor House Hotel for their first few days in the city, but he decided to move them across the creek to the Palace Hotel on the Bund, believing it to be a safer location.

After breakfast, they all checked out of the Astor. Taxicabs ferried them and their luggage through the rain across the Garden Bridge, along the Bund and onto the Nanking Road and the lobby of the Palace Hotel, directly across the road from the Cathay. The Palace was more costly than the Astor, but Reischauer planned to stay only one more day before continuing on to Tokyo. The additional safety of being in the heart of the International Settlement, rather than embattled Hongkew, was worth the expense of one night at the Palace. He was assigned a suite on the third floor, his bags were taken up and he settled into his room. He had some time to make notes and read before a meeting at 4.30 p.m.

Looking along the Bund at Shanghai close to where Chinese aeroplanes dropped bombs. The buildings which were hit included the Cathay Hotel, the Palace Hotel and the North China Daily News office, which are shown.

Photograph of the Bund in *The Age*, Monday, 16 August, 1937

Just Another Working Day

Shanghailanders generally worked a six-day week with Sundays off. Lucien Ovadia, a cousin of the wealthy businessman Sir Victor Sassoon, was at work in the offices of E.D. Sassoon & Co. on the third floor of Sassoon House, part of the complex fronting the Bund waterfront that included the swank Cathay Hotel. Ovadia was one of the vaunted *taipans* of Shanghai, the Big Bosses, who looked after the Sassoon firm's finances across the Far East. Born in Egypt he was of Spanish nationality, educated in France, had lived in London and travelled extensively throughout the Far East. It was often said of him that he was, almost, as cosmopolitan as Shanghai itself. Ovadia was working in his office with the windows open in order to catch the wind coming in from the Whangpoo River and take the edge off the stifling indoor humidity.

Frank J. Rawlinson, an American protestant missionary who had been in China since 1902 was now sixty-six years of age. Shanghai had been his home for thirty-five years. On Saturdays he invariably worked at the Missions Building on Yuan Ming Yuan Road, close to the Bund and just behind the British Consulate. Around thirty different missionary societies shared offices in the building and most worked on Saturdays 'spreading the word' across China.

American advertising agent Carl Crow was in his office down along the Bund on Jinkee Road, a short walk away from the Missions Building. Crow had arrived in China from Missouri just in time for the 1911 Republican revolution that overthrew the Qing Dynasty. He had become friends with Dr Sun Yat-sen, lived through China's Warlord Era and had been an active member of the SVC in 1932 during the last Japanese threat to Shanghai. He was a veteran China watcher and a stalwart of the American community in the Settlement. That morning he sat at his desk and worked on a report for one of his major clients, Colgate. He sought to assure them that, despite ongoing skirmishes with Japan in Northern China, the Yangtze Valley and Shanghai remained calm with stable business conditions. He reminded them that their China sales were growing and that other American companies were also prospering in the city's flourishing consumer market. He noted that sales of Kodak cameras, another of his major clients, were strong. For some time Crow had been considering whether to lease a beachfront property in the resort-city of Tsingtao as a holiday home to escape the humidity of oxygen-deprived Shanghai in summer. True, there had been some 'little squabbles' around the city – the current shelling of Chapei was one such – but there had been no major incidents.

He looked out of his window up at the storm-wracked skies over the narrow street below. Jinkee Road ran along the northern side of the Cathay Hotel, parallel with Nanking Road, and had transformed from a small

Carl Crow

Ellen Louise Schmid

lane of opium godowns into a street lined with modern office blocks populated by thriving foreign and Chinese commercial enterprises. Like Lucien Ovadia, Crow's biggest problem that morning was staying awake and maintaining concentration in the airless humidity.

Ellen Louise Schmid was standing on the roof terrace of the Cathay Hotel with her mother, Mary. Her Swiss father, Theodor (Theo), represented Anderson, Clayton in Shanghai, the world's largest cotton traders based in Oklahoma City. The Schmids had a beautiful house on Amherst Avenue, in Shanghai's leafier western district. Ellen had been raised in the Settlement and had written elegiac poems to the city as a young girl. Her life had been one of excitement. As well as living in the Far East's most modern and cosmopolitan city, her last trip back to America had been aboard the Zeppelin *Hindenburg* from

Eleanor B. Roosevelt & son Quentin

Germany to New York. She was now a senior at Stanford, back home visiting her parents for the summer. Her mother had taken her to the Cathay for *tiffin* as a treat. They stood on the roof of the hotel looking out across the Whangpoo, past the gunboats lining the river and over the marshlands out beyond the factories and godowns that crowded the Pootung shoreline on the opposite bank. Ellen's mother had brought her new camera.

Several floors below the Schmids, Eleanor B. Roosevelt, former American President Teddy Roosevelt's daughter-in-law, was dining with her son Quentin. They had arrived in Shanghai a couple of days before, having travelled from Nanking where Eleanor met with Madame Chiang. Eleanor knew the Far East intimately; her husband Theodore Roosevelt III, the former

President's oldest son, had been the Governor-General of the Philippines. Eleanor and nineteen-year-old Quentin were on a tour of the region. Quentin was interested in China, particularly in the Naxi people of Sichuan on whom he was planning to write a university paper. The two discussed their tour and considered a little sightseeing after lunch.

The ever-busy John Morris had spent Saturday morning back up on the roof of Broadway Mansions with Randall Gould. It offered one of the best views across northern Shanghai to survey the extent of the Japanese attack. Looking across to the Settlement it seemed every rooftop along the Bund was packed with people watching the skies that burned orange with the flames from Chapei. He noted the glinting reflection of dozens of pairs of binoculars. The Japanese attack on Chapei had become a spectator sport. Down along the Bund, close by the junction of the waterfront and the Settlement's major east-west artery of Nanking Road, he saw thousands of refugees. They had crossed the Garden Bridge out of Chapei and Hongkew seeking sanctuary from the Japanese attack. Together with a few curious Shanghailanders, they formed a cluster on the corner occupied by the massive Cathay Hotel, all looking skywards.

Overnight, Claire Lee Chennault had considered his pilots' lack of training and the adverse weather conditions, but had finally decided to go ahead with the mission. The first Chinese bombers took off from Lunghwa Aerodrome at around 10 a.m. Rhodes Farmer was standing on the roof of the *North-China Daily News* Building, known as the 'Old Lady of the Bund' at quarter past ten that morning. He watched five Chinese bombers fly towards the Whangpoo and the *Idzumo* at about five thousand feet in a tight 'V' formation. The *Idzumo*'s anti-aircraft guns opened up, and were joined by those on the other Japanese ships in a deafening roar. The five Chinese planes passed over the *Idzumo* heading north, up towards the Japanese military command bunker in Hongkew Park. At 11 a.m., and again shortly afterwards at 11.20 a.m., came two waves of CAF Curtiss Hawk's that flew straight into what Farmer described as 'an impenetrable wall of bursting shells'. Most held their course despite the bombardment. One released its bombs but they accidentally overshot and hit the Shanghai-Hongkew Wharf on the Pootung side of the river.

Londoner Charles Head, Chief Accountant of the wharf, was seriously injured by the bomb. Two of his Portuguese employees were similarly wounded by shrapnel while three of his Chinese workers were killed and another ten seriously hurt.

Vanya Oakes had gone to the *China Press* offices near Avenue Edward VII to file her impressions of

Chapei that dawn. She then joined some colleagues for coffee at the Palace Hotel on Nanking Road. They had finally persuaded her to move hotels and she decided to go back and pack immediately. As she tried to cross the Garden Bridge to the Astor, she found it heavy going against the stream of Chinese refugees fleeing Chapei for the central Settlement. As the bomb hit the Shanghai-Hongkew Wharf nearby Oakes was trapped on the bridge and thought her eardrums would burst.

The refugees had been squeezed into a funnel to cross the narrow Garden Bridge into the Settlement. As the *Idzumo*'s guns opened fire at 11 a.m., panic struck the crowd. Frightened refugees scrambled over their hastily dropped bundles in their attempts to get into the Settlement. Trying to move against the manic crowd, Oakes was pushed to the edge of the bridge and had to grab hold of the iron railings to avoid being swallowed up in the stampede or tipped into the creek. Several people were trampled to death in the panicked confusion; Oakes felt the breath squeezed out of her. As Rhodes Farmer also crossed the bridge, he 'slipped in blood and flesh' and felt the sickening crunch of the very young and the very old who had fallen under the waves of pushing refugees. The Japanese sentries were unable to control the situation and lashed out with their bayonets. Several older Chinese were stabbed. The sentries dumped the lifeless body of one bayoneted old man off the Garden Bridge and into the Soochow Creek below.

Vanya Oakes simply wasn't strong enough to push through the crowd. She changed direction and went back to the Bund side, hoping to get a sampan across Soochow Creek to the Astor. The river was, as usual, packed with sampans. She took off her high heels and started 'sampan hopping', jumping from one flimsy craft to another in the hope of making it to the other side.

More bombs fell as Oakes jumped from one boat to another, high heels and purse in hand, much to the amusement of the boat owners. She made it to the northern bank just as the 11.20 a.m. planes screeched in overhead. She quickly found shelter with a friendly boatman under the canvas awning of his sampan. Bombs fell towards Pootung and shrapnel from the Japanese anti-aircraft guns rained down, killing the occupants of one boat just fifty feet away. After the planes roared away, Oakes went ashore and into the Astor to pack her suitcase.

For those in their offices near the Bund like Lucien Ovadia, Carl Crow and Frank Rawlinson, they could feel the windows rattle in the morning bombing raids. First at 11 a.m. and then again at 11.20 a.m., they heard the Chinese bombers fly over, explosions and then the response of the *Idzumo*'s big guns. The roof of Rawlinson's Missions Building was crowded with spectators who covered their heads as shrapnel rattled down onto the roof. Charles Luther Boynton of the National Christian Council of Churches ordered everyone off the roof and then padlocked it to ensure the more curious didn't return. Frank Rawlinson consequently decided to get in his car and drive home to the French Concession for lunch with his family.

The Calm Before the Storm

The first bombing run had failed to score a hit on the *Idzumo*. Shanghai returned to normal for several hours and the skies remained clear. A.D. Williams counted himself lucky to be dining at the luxurious Cathay Hotel that Saturday. As the accountant for the *North-China Daily News*, he wasn't usually the one taken to lunch or drinks. He sat at his desk most days from nine to six, watching the journalists and editors saunter in and out all day from *tiffins*, dinners and Shanghai's great tradition of 'Sundowner' drinks. He saw their expenses, he knew how much of the company budget was spent on entertaining. But today, a major client of the paper had decided to buy the *North-China's* accountant lunch – it was he, after all, who could suddenly decide whether too much was being spent on newsprint or ink. Williams was being courted at one of the best restaurants in town and he was enjoying it.

Alongside the Cathay Hotel was Sassoon Arcade,

which housed a popular tea shop as well as some of Shanghai's finest and most expensive antique and curio stores. Above the retail premises were any number of important businesses including the busy offices of travel agents Thomas Cook, a Chinese government telegram office, American Express and the always crowded Mme. Verette Institute de Beauté. Tourists loved the arcade for its curio stores – the Green Dragon, the Peking Treasure Shop, Cathay Arts, Grays Yellow Lantern Shop run by husband and wife proprietors Bill and Dolly Gray, and especially Hoggard-Sigler, who specialised in very rare and terribly dear bronzes, brasses and Chinese art and *objets*. Saturdays were always busy for the shops and offices of Sassoon Arcade and this one was no exception.

For those Shanghailanders and tourists who were out shopping and enjoying late lunches or early cocktails after the morning's excitements, the second phase of Claire Lee Chennault's plan to sink the *Idzumo* came as a surprise. Many Chinese were still fleeing across the Garden Bridge from burning Chapei, and congregating on the Bund before they could disperse to various refugee centres in the Settlement and Frenchtown. For these poor souls the new assault was simply terrifying. At approximately 4 p.m. the *Idzumo* opened up its anti-aircraft guns once more and began firing two hundred feet into the sky, though no actual planes had yet been sighted.

At close to 4.30 p.m. Rhodes Farmer, still on the roof of the *North-China Daily News* Building, saw ten Northrop bombers with CAF markings appear over the Settlement. The leading six planes disappeared into low-hanging cloud coverage while the rear four veered off their course. Two bombs, and then a further two, fell from beneath one of the planes.

Farmer would later report that the typhoon winds had caught the bombs and were blowing them back towards the Settlement. He held his breath, thinking the bombs would hit the British destroyer nearby. They just missed. The first bomb hit the water and sent up a giant waterspout. The second bomb slammed into a cluster of fragile sampans and sprayed brown muddy water and boat parts up onto the Bund, wiping out their occupants completely. The next two bombs were due to land slightly further back across the Bund. Farmer knew then that he was '. . . dead centre in Asia's first blitz'. He stood transfixed as the bombs rained down towards the Palace and Cathay hotels, and the crowded junction of Nanking Road and the Bund.

Victor Keene, the *New York Tribune's* hard drinking and fun-loving Shanghai correspondent who also wrote for the local *China Press*, was on the roof of the American Club on Foochow Road, a block away from the Cathay. He watched the same formation of CAF Northrop bombers fly across the Settlement, noting that they were the planes that had been presented to Chiang Kai-shek on the occasion of his last birthday. Keene saw the anti-aircraft guns on the decks of the *Idzumo* open fire. The shrapnel fallout out was immediate and long range as it fell back earthwards, wounding a Chinese waiter standing next to him. Keene then saw four black dots appear below the planes – bombs, dislodged from their racks – that began falling towards the Settlement, short of their target. The first two slammed into the Whangpoo. Keene was aghast as he realised that the next two bombs were going to miss the *Idzumo* and fall towards the Bund. He immediately scrambled off the roof and headed towards Nanking Road.

Ellen Schmid and her mother stood on the roof of the Cathay and watched the Chinese planes fly over from the west and head towards the river and the great grey hulk of the *Idzumo*. They watched in horror as several bombs fell from the bottom of one of the bombers and:

> . . . drifted downward. Our eyes followed it down. There was a blinding flash. For a minute or two we couldn't see anything but the flash. Then flames and smoke shot up. The explosion was so loud we couldn't hear the anti-aircraft guns anymore. Just a few seconds later two more bombs fell. There were two more flashes and two more explosions. We ran inside.

Then for a few seconds, as Rhodes Farmer remembered, Shanghai went 'as silent as a morgue'.

The First Blast – 4.27 p.m.

The first bomb to hit the Settlement weighed 2000 lb and hit the Palace Hotel at precisely 4.27 p.m. It passed straight through the roof and plummeted downwards through the building. The hotel's tea lounge, restaurant, lobby and bar were all destroyed. Many of the dead and injured were found later, still in their rooms. Part of the Palace's façade had been blown away and had begun to collapse. One man, blown out of his room on the fourth floor, clung perilously to the edge of the building. Nobody could reach him and he eventually plummeted to the ground, smashing through the glass awning of the hotel entranceway and onto the pavement.

The second bomb struck seconds later bearing directly down on Nanking Road. It glanced off the side of the Cathay Hotel's ferroconcrete structure, cracked the canopy covering the entranceway and exploded into the tarmac. Shrapnel hit the clock on the front of the Cathay, which stopped at 4.27 p.m. exactly. The bomb left a gaping crater right outside the front doors. Always a busy intersection, the street instantly became a mass of burnt-out cars. Flames licked from a gutted Lincoln Zephyr parked near the hotel's entrance. Its whitewall tyres were still a brilliant white but the body

Site of the bombing near the Palace Hotel

Scene of the bombing between the Palace Hotel and the Cathay Hotel on Nanking Road

had been reduced to a chassis shell. Next to it stood a bicycle, standing upright as if waiting for its owner to return and claim it. Fallen telegraph poles and twisted streetcar wires amid a sea of broken plate glass created barriers across the road. Loosened masonry from the Palace and the Cathay fell at random points. Blinding acrid smoke and, after a momentary silence in the wake of the bomb, the screams of the injured and dying rose up. A fire blazed.

The Bund end of Nanking Road was carnage. Dead and dismembered bodies littered the street. Charred corpses had been flung by the blast as far as the waterfront, landing on the dead who moments before had been clustered together watching the skies above. Seven hundred, overwhelmingly Chinese, refugees had been crowded around the waterfront junction, seeking shelter from the rain and winds. Many died instantly; others were horribly injured. Percy Finch, the veteran City Editor of the *North-China Daily News*, had been on the roof of the newspaper's building just along the Bund.

It seemed as if a giant mower had pushed through the crowd of refugees, chewing them to bits. Here was a headless man; there a baby's foot, wearing its little red-silk shoe embroidered with fierce dragons. Bodies were piled in heaps by the capricious force of the explosions. Women still clutched their precious bundles. One body, that of a young boy, was flattened high against a wall, to which it clung with ghastly adhesion.

Carl Crow was putting the final touches to his report for Colgate, hoping to catch the last post. He was planning to finish up his day's work and head to the American Club, where he was Treasurer, for a few whisky sodas and maybe a game of Texas Hand Poker before returning home to his wife Helen and their villa house on well-healed Connaught Road. He never finished the report. The windows in his office blew out as the first bomb exploded outside the Cathay one street away. Miraculously none of the shattering glass cut him as he ducked under his desk. He recalled hearing the sound of machine gunfire ripping through the air, followed by a burst of shrapnel from an anti-aircraft gun somewhere nearby. He assumed it came from the *Idzumo* just across the river. Getting up, Crow peered out of his shattered window to see mayhem on the street below. Filling the scene were abandoned rickshaws, wheel-barrows and terrified citizens running for cover.

He wasn't the only cowering businessman. In the next building, Canadian insurance broker Martin Gold was sitting at his desk when a massive lump of shrapnel blew out the window and missed his head by an inch. A.D. Williams stepped out the front door of the Cathay Hotel and shook hands with his lunch host who retreated back inside to his suite. He stood on the street outside and lit a cigarette, turning down towards the Old Lady of the Bund and his office with the desk, files, blotters, ledgers and adding machinery. He looked up at the clock that hung over the entrance of the hotel lobby. It said 4.27 p.m. Williams was killed instantly as the bomb landed almost directly on top of him.

Rhodes Farmer walked down several flights of stairs as the Old Lady of the Bund's elevators had stopped working. He then grabbed his Chinese photographer from under the darkroom table and they rushed along the waterfront to Nanking Road. At the junction, Farmer encountered a decapitated Sikh Shanghai Municipal Police officer '. . . with his arms outstretched as though against oncoming traffic'. Looking up Nanking Road towards the entrance of the Cathay, Farmer saw

. . . Flames from blazing cars incinerating the bodies of their riddled occupants. In grotesque heaps where they had been huddling in doorways and annexes of the Cathay and Palace Hotels were heaps of refugees whose blue coolie clothes were turning red. Heads, arms, legs lay far from mangled trunks. For the full long stretch of both buildings, the pavements and roadway were littered with bodies.

Lucien Ovadia was hurled across the room 'like a rag doll'

by the second blast that had glanced the Cathay. He was lucky that his windows had been open and the blast hadn't sent deadly shards of glass flying back into the room. He sat on the floor, stunned, for a minute or two. Then amazingly, given the devastation of the office around him, his telephone rang. It was Louis Suter, the Swiss manager of the Cathay, wishing to inform him that a bomb had fallen and destroyed the hotel's canopy. Ovadia went down in the still working elevator and exited Sassoon House into Sassoon Arcade.

The arcade was devastated. The windows of Grays Yellow Lantern shop had been completely blown out. Priceless Chinese *objets d'art* and expensive items of Lalique glassware were smashed on the floor amid bits of flesh and blood. All the shops in the arcade, including Alexander Clark's jewellers on the first floor and the Western Union offices, were badly damaged and many staff were wounded. Hoggard-Sigler was seriously damaged. Intricate ivory carvings, ruby red Peking glass bowls, beautiful statues of the Goddess Guanyin, jade ornaments, lacquer furniture and silk brocades had all been destroyed. The proprietor, Clarence Hoggard, would never be able to open the store again. Fortunately, a party of twenty-four visiting schoolteachers, who had been taking tea in the arcade shortly before the bomb fell, had set off to explore Shanghai's old town and had just missed the explosion.

After the Initial Shock

Rhodes Farmer felt the 'sticky sweet stench of blood' in his nostrils. Across the tramlines that ran down Nanking Road to the Bund was the body of a tall European in a white suit – the suit was still immaculate though his head had been cleanly sliced off. He saw petrified tourists still sitting at their seats in the Palace's cocktail lounge, which had somehow escaped destruction. A colleague, who had only earlier asked him to go for a drink at the Palace, lay dead on his back, staring sightlessly towards the sky. Two Russian men helped Farmer lift the body by the shoulders, but a terrible stomach wound made it impossible. Farmer began to help carry the wounded in from the street, fearing that the bombers might return.

Farmer and the two Russians tried to carry a young man with dark hair into the Palace. His leg had been severely injured and he was unconscious. Farmer attempted to drag him through the revolving doors of the Palace, but they were jammed with broken glass. The men began to smash out some street-facing windows to get him inside. Farmer realised that it was Robert Reischauer, who he had interviewed only two days before. As soon as the first ambulances arrived, Reischauer was rushed to hospital, but he died a few hours later from a combination of shock and blood loss. The remainder of his party were mostly playing bridge in the hotel and had survived. Paul Amos, another

Princeton academic in the party, had gone for a stroll along the Bund and had missed the blast. He ran back to the hotel to see 'the street lined with bleeding bodies, torn and mangled. Huge slivers of glass fell to the street from windows.'

United Press correspondents Bud Ekins and John Morris were just around the corner from the Cathay at their office. The very border of the Settlement and the French Concession was the Avenue Edward VII, known to all Shanghailanders as the 'Avenue Eddy'. The concentrated strip of press offices on the street was known locally as 'Newspaper Alley'. After covering the fighting in Chapei for forty-eight hours straight, Ekins and Morris had decided to take a late and well-deserved lunch at the Cathay. Morris had then stayed in the Cathay to interview some guests while Ekins went across to the Palace Hotel to meet some other journalists he knew and try to work out why the *Idzumo's* anti-aircraft guns were firing at an apparently empty sky. Morris was in the lobby of the Cathay about to leave; Ekins was in the lobby of the Palace. Both were about to step out onto the street; both escaped sudden death by seconds. Morris was forced to jump through a broken plate glass window to exit the lobby of the Cathay since the front entrance was blocked by the destroyed canopy. He saw their car with the front wheels blown off and assumed Ekins must have been killed along with their driver Wang. Morris was moved and wrote up his report, which was cabled back across the Pacific that night. Thanks to the international dateline, he made the late editions of the American newspapers,

> I saw a white woman, kneeling in the blood and wreckage
> of Nanking Road, trying to aid her daughter in giving
> birth to a child as bullets, bomb fragments and debris
> flew about.

Ekins hadn't been killed, and neither had Wang, who had gone for a walk while his boss was in the hotel. He had clambered out of the wrecked lobby of the Palace to help Morris report the devastation. Morris was covered in plaster and window glass and later reported that the explosions had been accompanied by ear-splitting noise. He looked out of the smashed window at the devastation on Nanking Road,

> I could see at least fifty persons writhing on the sidewalks
> and roadway. Three foreigners were trying to crawl away
> over the bodies of the dead Chinese.

Victor Keene had arrived from the American Club and stood outside the Palace Hotel. He watched the injured doorman crawl towards the reception desk before he himself recoiled from another explosion caused by a fractured gas main. The blast sent up a geyser of dust and debris, killing many of the injured on the street outside who were unable to scramble away in time. Keene tried to call for ambulances from the Palace's lobby telephones, but the lines were dead. He then tried to attend to some of the wounded in the lobby. He saw a stunned R.E. Rasche, a Swiss who worked for the local Union brewery in Shanghai, outside on the street with a bad head injury, slumped up against the wall of the hotel next to his friend and colleague Max Jakoby whose leg had been severed in the blast. Keene tried to help Rasche to his feet. All the Swiss man could say was, 'I guess that's the last of Jakoby.' Rasche's colleague was dead.

Ekins and Morris, along with their driver Wang, Victor Keene and Rhodes Farmer, moved among the dead and injured, trying to identify them. Keene counted forty bodies between the front door of the Cathay and the Bund waterfront; Morris counted one hundred in less than a block – 'Some had their heads and arms blown off. Other lay with torn, twitching faces.' The men tried to assist a foreigner who had had half his face blown away in the explosion, and then they helped an old Chinese man load his wounded son onto a handcart, now a makeshift ambulance, in the hope of getting him to a hospital in time.

Police and ambulances rushed to Nanking Road but they were simply overwhelmed by the number of people needing treatment. The scene within the Palace Hotel was one of carnage, wreaked by the bomb as it had travelled downwards through the building. Herr Boss, the Palace's Swiss manager, shouted for ambulances. He had found dead and injured guests in many rooms – six seriously wounded people in one room alone – but there was little that could be done. Sections of the hotel were ablaze. Fire engines arrived with bells clanging and worked to put out the flames before they engulfed the entire building.

John Morris reported that the ambulance crews had to make the awful choice of only treating those who had a chance of living. There were just too many wounded who needed treatment. Many died by the side of Nanking Road and in the surrounding laneways and alleys for want of medical attention. The first co-ordinated response came half an hour later when a company of British Army armoured cars pushed through the crowds, bringing officers who set up a field hospital for the wounded and gathered up the dead. Many of the injured had to wait for the arrival of the armoured car before they could be treated. John Morris recalled seeing a friend of his, the popular Geordie and long-time China resident, John Findlay from Newcastle, waiting patiently for the ambulances in the devastated lobby of the Cathay Hotel. Wounded himself, Findlay spent his time comforting other injured guests, reassuring them that they would be all right and that more ambulances were coming.

The municipal ambulances and firemen were soon joined by volunteers from the Chinese Red Cross and Red Swastika (Buddhist) societies. Rhodes Farmer watched one Chinese nurse tending the wounded, '. . . her white uniform quickly becoming as red as the badge on her arm'. He also saw a Japanese girl in high heels and western clothes, standing under the dead hands of the Cathay's clock, directing the rescue parties towards any wounded on the street who could be saved.

Lucien Ovadia and the management of the Cathay moved through the hotel, evacuating the one hundred and fifty guests still in their rooms, as well as others who had been dining in the hotel. Those ushered to safety included a shocked Ellen Schmid and her mother, who had been on the roof taking photos when the bombs fell. Also among those escorted to safety were Eleanor B. Roosevelt and her son Quentin. After surveying the carnage outside, Eleanor urgently sought to make her way immediately to the American Consulate. As they stepped out of the entrance near the Sassoon Arcade, hotel staff kindly told them to take care – there was a four-foot deep shell crater in the pavement.

The SVC organised a convoy of commandeered furniture removal trucks to take the dead away. Rhodes Farmer, his white linen summer suit now covered in blood, was still at the scene and watched the young men of the SVC begin the grim task of gathering up the bodies. Farmer noted that the boys '. . . vomited into the gutter, then grinned self-consciously and got on with their grisly tasks'. Percy Finch grabbed the exhausted Farmer and told him he had done all he could and to come for a drink to steel his nerves.

Finch and Farmer walked into the wrecked Cathay and were amazed to find the Horse and Hounds bar still open. Farmer remembers the Chinese stewards producing a bottle of brandy and then recoiling when another drinker, a White Russian man, bent down from his stool, picked up a thumb from the floor, held it out and asked, 'Any of you lose this?'

Many of the survivors from Nanking Road came under the care of Dr D.B. Cater at the modern Lester Chinese Hospital. Cater was a well-known, Cambridge-educated junior surgeon. After lecturing in pathology at Cambridge, Cater and his family had moved to Shanghai to work in the newly built six-storey, three hundred-bed hospital. Located on Shantung Road just a few blocks back from the Bund, it was the largest hospital in the vicinity of the Nanking Road blast site. The scale of the catastrophe quickly overwhelmed the Lester's facilities.

Cater claimed the hospital was 'swamped' with injured people lying on floors and out in the hospital's courtyards.

By early evening, Cater and his team of surgeons had lost count of the number of amputations they had performed. For those of whom no surgery or care could help, morphine was given to ease the pain.

Other prominent Shanghailanders died in the blast outside the Cathay Hotel. An early tally of the dead included Reischauer, Williams, two Germans and a further two Russians, one of whom was identified as a man called Walter Turpin. A German guest at the Cathay had his leg torn off below the knee and bled to death; another guest sitting in the lobby was flung from his chair, slammed against a wall and killed. Among the injured survivors were J.M. Kerbey, who worked in Shanghai for the New York accountants Haskins and Sells, who was wounded by shrapnel outside the Palace Hotel. Montanan R.R. Rouse, a 44-year-old former Marine, was with his wife and daughter when he took shrapnel to his left shoulder and knee while in the passenger seat of his car near the Cathay. His wife and daughter, as well as the baby's Chinese *amah* and Rouse's Chinese chauffeur were unharmed despite the windscreen and all the windows in the car being blown out by the blast.

The number of Chinese dead was clearly large, but unverified – both in the total number and their individual names. Many, it seems, had been wounded by the blasts, crawled into the side streets and died anonymously.

Victor Keene helped to transport the wounded to hospital. Beyond the Lester, the nearest hospital was across the border in the French Concession – the Chinese Hospital on Thibet Road. Keene helped to load some wounded Chinese into a functioning car owned by a Canadian Shanghailander Dr W.S. Parsons who had been in the Palace Hotel. They set off towards Frenchtown, only to drive straight into another hell.

The Second Bomb – 4.43 p.m.

A second group of bombs fell at 4.43 p.m. approximately fifteen minutes after the first two exploded in Nanking Road. This time they struck at the corner of Thibet Road and the Avenue Eddy, right outside the Great World amusement palace. It was the French Concession's busiest junction. The pavements around the entertainment complex were, as ever, thronged with the curious.

The Great World, the *Da Shijie*, had opened in 1917, though the magnificent Baroque-style building topped by a four-storey tower wasn't completed until 1928. It was a Shanghai landmark, a first stop for Chinese visitors from out of town and foreign sojourners alike. It was akin to a London pleasure garden, spread across six floors and a large open roof space overlooking one of the most densely populated parts of the French Concession. Having visited several years earlier, the Hollywood movie director Josef von Sternberg described the scene he encountered at the Great World,

On the first floor were gaming tables, singsong girls, magicians, pick-pockets, slot machines, fireworks, birdcages, fans, stick incense, acrobats, and ginger. One flight up were the restaurants, a dozen different groups of actors, crickets and cages, pimps, midwives, barbers, and earwax extractors. The third floor had jugglers, herb medicines, ice cream parlors, a new bevy of girls, their high collared gowns slit to reveal their hips, and, under the heading of novelty, several rows of exposed toilets. The fourth floor was crowded with shooting galleries, fan-tan tables, revolving wheels, massage benches, acupuncture and moxa cabinets, hot towel counters, dried fish and intestines, and dance platforms . . . The fifth floor featured girls with dresses slit to the armpits, a stuffed whale, storytellers, balloons, peep shows, masks, a mirror maze, two love letter booths with scribes who guaranteed results, rubber goods, and a temple filled with ferocious gods and joss sticks. On the top floor and roof of that house of multiple joys a jumble of tightrope walkers slithered back and forth, and there were seesaws, Chinese

checkers, mahjong, strings of firecrackers, lottery
tickets, and marriage brokers.

This weekend the crowds thronging the Great World were added to by the fact that the ground floor had been converted into an emergency refugee centre for five thousand Chinese who had fled the bombardment of Chapei and Kiangwan. Charitable organisations were handing out free bowls of rice and tea, which swelled the numbers yet further. Rhodes Farmer, who had walked from Nanking Road round to the Great World to carry on reporting, noted the irony that many of those seeking shelter had contributed to the collection boxes at the Great World for the Chinese government's 'Buy-A-Bomber' fund drive. It was apparent by then the bombs had fallen from a Chinese plane and had not come from the *Idzumo's* guns.

An initially widely accepted belief surrounding the bombing of the Settlement was that a Chinese pilot, crippled by anti-aircraft fire from the *Idzumo*, had intended to limp back to Lunghwa, jettisoning his bombs on the nearby expanse of the racecourse en route. If that was the case then his miscalculation proved to be horrendously deadly.

The first bomb detonated shortly before hitting the ground, sending out a spray of deadly eviscerating shrapnel that killed people over seven hundred yards

Bomb crater in front of the Great World

away. The second bomb hit the asphalt street and created a huge crater, ten feet by six, adjacent to a traffic control tower.

The bombs that exploded outside the Great World were more deadly than the first wave in Nanking Road. There was a greater concentration of people in the area and the bombs were made of shrapnel, which accounted for the high casualty rate at the Great World. The shrapnel spread across a wide arc, reaching as far as the racecourse where stray pieces of boiling hot metal caused the immediate cessation of a cricket game underway at the time.

South African reporter Henry John May, out interviewing refugees from Chapei, was just fifty yards from the front door of the Great World when the bomb struck. He was blown off his feet, thrown onto his back and winded. He gathered his breath and stood up, realising that many of the Chinese refugees he had just been talking to at the base of the building had been killed on impact. Many injuries had been rendered fatal by the intense gas pressure from the explosions; some bodies had simply evaporated.

After lunch with his family in their Frenchtown home, missionary Frank Rawlinson took a drive to get a newspaper, as was his regular Saturday afternoon habit. His wife Florence, and fifteen-year-old daughter Jean, decided to accompany him. They passed close to the Great World on their way home and encountered the crowds of Chapei and Kiangwan refugees outside. Rawlinson, always keen to help, slowed the car. Florence suggested he get out to see what was happening. Rawlinson was in the midst of stepping out of the front passenger seat when the first bomb dropped. He was immediately hit in the chest by flying shrapnel that pierced his heart and killed him instantly. His wife pulled him back into the vehicle, took the wheel herself and drove to the foreign mortuary. As well as their daughter Jean, the Rawlinsons had six older children back in America.

Brooklyn-born Bernhard 'Bert' Covit, a former newspaperman himself with the *New York Post*, witnessed the bombing at the Great World, having arrived at the junction of Avenue Eddy and Thibet Road just after the two bombs fell.

Bert Covit told the press that the area around the Great World was a mass of shrieking and terrified Chinese, '. . . windows for blocks around were shattered'. He waited for the fire and police services to arrive and then helped them load the dead, who '. . . looked mummified and inhuman'. Among the mostly Chinese dead he noted several blond heads.

One of the burnt out cars was 'crushed like egg shells', said the journalist M.C. Ford, Shanghai correspondent for the *Chicago Daily News*. Inside were the remains of sixty-year-old Hubert Honigsberg, a pioneer San Franciscan Studebaker dealer who had become extremely wealthy from the city's infatuation with the motorcar. Like Rawlinson, he had been driving past the Great World when the bombs struck. Flying red-hot shrapnel ignited the petrol tank of his car, incinerating him. Police were only able to identify his body later through documents in what was left of the glove compartment. Also in the car was the body of a woman passenger. She remained unidentified for several days until it was determined that the horrifically-charred corpse was that of Honigsberg's wife, Madeleine.

Brother Shull, who managed the publishing activities of the Seventh Day Adventist Mission in Shanghai, was arriving in his car outside their printing presses virtually opposite the Great World. He saw the line of destroyed cars with the bodies still inside. Leaving his own, he walked through the devastation on the street to the mission's premises. It was a grisly scene. Some ninety Chinese printers, out of a staff of a hundred, who printed the Seventh Day Adventist Mission magazine, had been killed in the blast.

Having driven past exploding vehicles that sent up sheets of flame on Nanking Road, Victor Keene was in one of the luckier cars passing the Great World when the bombs exploded. His car, carrying injured Chinese to the hospital just a hundred yards from the Great World, was unharmed and he managed to deliver the wounded to the hospital which was about to become overwhelmed by the injured from the Frenchtown blasts. Keene assumed that the number of casualties would be even greater at the Great World than on Nanking Road. He knew the open rooftop had been a popular site to watch the circling planes and the fires in Chapei. He also knew it had become a refugee centre for Chinese fleeing northern Shanghai who had made it into the Settlement. He tried not to think about how many might have perished.

Keene doubled back to the Great World to report on the disaster. He also noted the crushed cars and the number of dead on the street outside. Keene was angry at the Chinese, and asked why they had bombed the

Settlement. He believed that the attacks on the Cathay and Great World were targeted to provocatively lure the foreign powers of the Settlement into the fight with Japan. He couldn't understand the attack on the Great World given that the refugees within had moved south of Soochow Creek on the explicit advice of the Chinese government. He couldn't believe it was all just an awful accident.

Vanya Oakes had checked out of the Astor House Hotel as planned and was in the large Huxinting teahouse in the old town's Yu Yuan Gardens, close to the French Concession, when she heard the explosions. The bombs sounded awfully close and she headed in the direction of the Great World thinking it was the racecourse that had been hit by a crash-landing plane. On the corner of Avenue Eddy and Thibet Road she encountered pandemonium. She stumbled towards the blast crater on Thibet Road and watched water from a broken pipe shoot upwards as blood washed across the street and trickled into the crater. She joined the rescue effort and was told, 'Look for those who are breathing – leave the others for now.'

Facing the Slaughter House

R. Somers from the Central Fire Station was in charge of the first engine that reached the Great World. He told Rhodes Farmer that, 'A call came through to the station. I hadn't got the faintest notion of what had happened although I coupled matters with the explosions I had heard.' As he arrived aboard his engine, Somers recalled, 'Facing that slaughter house there wasn't even time to rub my eyes. The cries told me I wasn't dreaming.' He jumped from the engine and ran back across to the Settlement side of Avenue Eddy to find a telephone and call the Chief Officer for more ambulances. He found a shop with a public phone that still worked. The front windows had been blown out and the customers inside were horrifically injured. Somers realised he had no change to make the call and saw among the few survivors a man whose limbs has been fatally damaged. He could think of nothing to do but ask the man for change. The man reached into his jacket pocket with his one good arm and handed Somers a five cent coin. Somers thanked him and turned to make the call. After requesting more ambulances, Somers turned back to the man to see if he could help him, but he had died.

The streets to the south of Avenue Eddy were in the French Concession and so it was the French *gendarmes* that responded to the tragedy first. Those at the recently built and very modern Mallet Station, the Poste Mallet, on Avenue Eddy realised immediately where the bomb had hit and were quick to arrive on the scene. *Gendarmes* from French Police HQ on

Route Stanislas Chevalier arrived soon after, including Nicolai Slobodchikoff. Outside on the bombed street he encountered 'crowds' of corpses on the pavement around the Great World.

Shortly after Slobodchikoff and other French *gendarmes* reached the scene, a division of the SVC's Russian Company arrived from the Avenue Joffre Fire Station. Among them was young Boris Ivanovich, who still had no uniform but had borrowed a tin helmet. Marching at the double down from the Avenue Joffre to Thibet Road, Ivanovich walked past the Metropole Cinema, where he had been sitting watching a Hollywood western the previous evening. The lobby of the cinema was now a hastily assembled refuge for the injured and dying. Joined by the Chinese company of the SVC, who had been barracked not far from the Great World at the Cathedral Boy's School, the police and Volunteers began to sort the wounded from the dead, and the hopeless cases from those who might have a chance of survival if they could get treatment.

Together Slobodchikoff and Ivanovich commandeered a French Concession flatbed garbage truck and loaded twenty-one badly wounded Chinese onto it. By the time they found a hospital able to take them, all but five had died. Slobodchikoff and Ivanovich were instructed to take the bodies to a cemetery in Siccawei, on the western fringes of the Concession, and bury them in a hastily dug mass grave. The two men were tasked with bringing some dignity to the dead by matching body parts to make whole bodies. It was a gruesome job and Slobodchikoff recalled the excruciating smell. When Slobodchikoff finally got back to French Police HQ his commanding inspector was shocked to see him covered in blood and white as a ghost. He poured him a shot of rum.

Word of the blasts spread fast across the city. George Stewart who worked for the Hong Kong and Shanghai Bank was sitting in the bar at the Race Club, a large clock tower that afforded a view of the east, encompassing the racecourse and the Great World. He heard a deafening bang and the clock tower shook. Someone who had been standing on a balcony and seen the Chinese planes passing overhead shouted, 'The bastards have dropped it.' Minutes later Stewart's acquaintance Harold Reynell, a First World War veteran, came into the bar for a stiffening drink. He had been in the traffic jam outside the Great World when the bombs hit but somehow his car had avoided combustion. His Chinese chauffeur had got them out of the area quickly and Reynolds had instructed him to head straight for the Race Club.

The socialite, author, *New Yorker* correspondent and general girl-about-town Emily 'Mickey' Hahn was across the Settlement on the far western Yu Yuen Road, where she was house-sitting for friends who had evacuated to Hong Kong. She was close to the western edge of the

Settlement, but even there occasionally, '. . . a little shrapnel fell into the garden or onto the roof'. Shortly after the explosions, Mickey met a Chinese friend who said he had been close by and had left the scene after seeing the bodies of several people he knew. She couldn't think what to say in reply.

The combined bombs on Nanking Road and the Great World on Bloody Saturday were the most devastating aerial attacks on a civilian city to that date in history and registered the highest casualty toll yet on record.

The Immediate Aftermath

As the afternoon moved into evening, rainy squalls periodically dampened the city and murky dark clouds continued to hover. Shanghai's hospitals were full to bursting. Workmen began converting several of the Settlement's dancehalls and ballrooms into makeshift treatment centres. Many Chinese women arrived at these centres, in *cheongsams* and high heels, but prepared to roll bandages and dress wounds. Most Shanghailanders were treated at the Country Hospital on the Great Western Road to the west of the city. Chinese found beds and treatment where they could; many more simply went home to be cared for. Facilities were stretched. The sanatorium of the Seventh Day Adventist Mission in the exposed Western External Roads, just beyond the Settlement's boundaries, was evacuated.

The sanatorium's thirty-five staff and thirty-four patients were distributed around the Settlement's increasingly overcrowded hospitals. The exclusive Columbia Country Club, with its swimming pool and rattan furniture where Shanghailanders had sipped cocktails only the day before, was rapidly converted into a military hospital.

The Japanese response to the bombs on Nanking Road and the Great World was to launch a barrage of shells from the *Idzumo* directly into Chapei, starting numerous fires once again. They must have known that all the Settlement's available ambulances and fire engines were attending the two devastated bombsites. Chapei was left without any help that Bloody Saturday evening.

Map of the war front in *Newcastle News*, Saturday, 14 August 1937

With all available police at the major bombsites, an orgy of looting began across Chapei, Hongkew and down towards Yangtzepoo. The skeleton crews of police left manning the Shanghai Municipal Police posts north of Soochow Creek were powerless to stop the plunder. Some households raised British and American flags in the hope that the looters would pass their properties by. Some displayed Nazi swastikas to indicate they were German households. This was a popular tactic for those Shanghailanders stuck behind the lines.

American George Battey lived in the Kiangwan area, a scene of serious fighting between Japanese and Chinese troops and artillery. He hoisted a Stars and Stripes outside his house. Despite being six feet two inches tall, Battey clambered into his five-foot iron bathtub with a loaf of bread and a tin of salmon when the shooting started. Battey was an optimistic man, who had worked on Chinese newspapers since 1931 and tried to live a Chinese lifestyle away from the more westernised Settlement. He had rather outraged British Shanghailander opinion by writing a book on the abdication of Edward VIII that praised Wallis Simpson, herself a former Shanghai sojourner. Although bullets passed through the plaster walls of his house and pinged off his iron bathtub, he avidly maintained that both sides had avoided deliberately shooting at his house and his flag. But when the firing quietened in the evening, he pumped up the tyres on his bicycle, strapped his typewriter, shaving kit and some personal belongings to the back, and stuck Old Glory on a pole attached to the back wheel. He then rode four miles through the skirmishing soldiers in northern Shanghai to the American Consulate, cutting a rather bizarre figure clad only in a bathing costume and khaki shorts.

Other Shanghailanders in the contested northern districts had their own stories to tell. Abijah Upson Fox, a well-known broker in the city for the New York firm of Swan, Culbertson & Fritz, was sitting in his apartment with his heavily pregnant wife Isabel. They had only been married eighteen months. A six-inch unexploded shell burst through the apartment's window, shot across the room and landed next to Isabel. Abijah jumped up, ran to his wife, picked up the shell and threw it back out through the window into the garden, burning his hands badly in the process.

The Chinese Red Cross, missionary societies and other charities were overwhelmed with lost and abandoned children separated from their parents in the chaos of the fighting and the exodus across Soochow Creek. It was reported that some Chinese parents were offering to sell their babies for as low as three shillings if they could be taken to a safe area.

In Hongkew, Japanese residents in Little Tokyo formed militias. They claimed to be under attack from the

Chinese, but the reality was that they were encouraged by the Japanese Army to randomly attack any Chinese civilians they found on the streets. They patrolled Hongkew armed with clubs that they were quick to use on any Chinese found on the streets. Fearing an aerial attack on Hongkew, the mobs smashed the streetlights to enforce their own blackout of the area.

The Japanese general headquarters were based in Hongkew Park; their frontline was at Jukong Road to the north and along the North Szechuen Road to the south, close to Soochow Creek. Japanese armoured cars patrolled the North Szechuen Road. The Chinese crack Eighty-Seventh Division was headquartered in the recently completed modernist Civic Centre in Kiangwan, which was under constant fire and pock-marked with shell damage.

The renewed Japanese bombardment of northern Shanghai was fuelled by mortar batteries in Hongkew Park, which illuminated the city as Saturday evening approached. Japanese Vice-Admiral Kiyoshi Hasegawa, Commander-in-Chief of all Japanese forces in Shang-hai, issued a declaration stating, 'The Japanese Navy is taking due action in view of the provocative actions of the Chinese.'

They mainly targeted the area around the North Railway Station, but a direct hit on the facility of the British-owned Asiatic Petroleum Company, mid-way between the Settlement and Woosung, lit the sky bright orange before clouds of black smoke poured over the Settlement. The burned gasoline was estimated at a value of US$5 million.

The Chinese Army continued to fight back, including the elite division that had been under Chiang Kai-shek's personal command, the Eighty-Seventh, the German-trained Eighty-Eighth Central Division, as well as the Thirty-Sixth Division. Radio station X.H.M.A. reported that every train into the city was bringing more Chinese Nationalist troops. As night fell, the streets of northern Shanghai became eerily empty. People avoided the threat from Chinese and Japanese snipers duelling it out across the rooftops.

Many Chinese died in northern Shanghai from ricochets, splinters and shrapnel. A renewed wave of Chinese refugees from Chapei turned into a tsunami – in cars, trucks, bicycles and with handcarts – approaching the Garden Bridge and the entrance onto the Bund and into the heart of the Settlement.

Randall Gould had stayed put in his Broadway Mansions watchtower to observe the shelling of Chapei and the bombs that fell on the Settlement, reporting all that he saw. Despite the chaos, he could see into the Settlement, down onto the Bund at the end of Nanking Road where the Cathay Hotel stood. He noticed that a growing flood of refugees was pouring out of Chapei,

Refugees fleeing Hongkew via the Garden bridge

through Hongkew and attempting to cross the Garden Bridge into what they believed would be the safety of the Settlement. Moving quickly to catch the fading light of the day, Gould took his camera and snapped the refugees crowding across the Bridge and onto the Bund, capturing what would later become one of the most iconic photos of the summer war in Shanghai.

More refugees from Paoshan and the western part of Chapei attempted to cross into the Settlement further west along the creek, via the Markham Road Bridge guarded by the US Fourth Marines. In addition to the human tide that was flowing over the Garden Bridge, Soochow Creek was being blocked by hundreds of flimsy sampans, offering to ferry refugees, for a price, from the north bank to the south bank. Colonel Charles F.B. Price went along the creek on an inspection tour and ordered his Marines to spread out from Markham Road and line the entire three-mile long bank to control the flow of refugees along the waterway. Additional refugee centres were established in the Settlement and Frenchtown, though food shortages were immediately apparent. Most restaurants, cinemas, theatres and shops opted to close for the evening.

Rhodes Farmer had finished his long day back at the Horse and Hounds bar at the Cathay and had to walk home as the city's rickshaw pullers stayed indoors. He tramped back across the Settlement where hastily adapted garbage trucks, converted furniture wagons, dozens of Chinese handcarts and overworked ambulances passed him by. They were carrying the dead away. Near the racecourse, and not far from the Great World, Farmer took a short cut through one of Shanghai's legion of narrow *lilong* laneways,

It was pitch dark on one side; whitened by the moon on the other. On the darkened side hundreds of people lay outstretched. Poor devils of homeless refugees sleeping it out, I thought. Funny, though, that none of them were stirring! Then a streetlight showed me what they were: the unburied dead. My lungs were bursting and my clothes dripped sweat when I had finished running from that open-air morgue.

Lucien Ovadia had stayed at the Cathay all evening trying to co-ordinate the clean-up operation and rescue effort. Despite appearances, the structural damage to the Cathay was relatively light, certainly compared to the devastation of the Palace Hotel across the street, which had taken a direct hit. Ovadia arranged with the manager Louis Suter, and his assistant Robert Telfer, to ensure the front of the hotel and its broken windows were boarded up. Workmen were hired to clean the façade of the hotel – remnants of the blast, including human blood and tissue, had smeared the building up as high as the fifth and sixth floors.

Ovadia then arranged with the Chinese Company of the SVC to guard the neighbouring Sassoon Arcade and its many antique stores. Despite the damage to the front, all the hotel's services, including its telephone system, hot water, restaurants and the Horse and Hounds bar were open again for business by the evening. Guests could still feel the crunch of broken glass beneath their shoes and had to avert their eyes from the blood on the street outside.

Vanya Oakes had left the Great World blast site after the police, firemen and SVC units turned up. Walking towards Nanking Road she had seen trucks, laden with the dead, coming from the direction of the Cathay Hotel. She realised the other bombs had been in that vicinity. She found the last of the body count being cleared from the rubble along Nanking Road and the Bund while burnt-out cars had been shunted aside to make room for trucks and fire engines to get through. She clambered over debris to get into the lounge of the Palace Hotel where she had had coffee with her *China Press* colleagues just a few hours before.

It was dark now and everything seemed closed, the street deserted. '. . . Against the walls of the hotel there were stacks of bodies, like sacks of wheat on a wharf. And – not one living soul in sight'.

R. Somers spent most of the rest of the day at the Great World. He eventually took his engine back to the Central Fire Station. There he found most of his colleagues looking deathly tired and trying to type up their reports while the day's events and horrific statistics were still fresh in their minds. He recalled that at intervals they would get up from their typewriters, go to the lavatory and vomit, then return and begin typing again.

Somers' father had been a surgeon, while he himself had attended many fires and seen his fair share of gruesome sights. He had long believed himself to be inured to the horrors of devastating blazes and deadly explosions. While he managed not to be sick he admitted that he had never before seen anything close to the terrible scenes he had witnessed that day on Thibet Road.

A City Never the Same Again

The last bomb seemed to have fallen that day, but people didn't stop panicking. The reliable safety of the International Settlement, outfitted with its own police and soldiers to protect the enclaves, had been permanently shattered. Many residents wanted to leave.

The Robert Dollar Line steamship *President Taft* was at anchor off the port awaiting permission to enter, while the *President Hoover* was just offshore, downriver at Woosung. Thousands of Shanghailanders crowded outside the Dollar Line offices on the Bund, trying to secure berths on ships that were already full and whose arrivals, let alone disembarkations, remained uncertain. The Dollar Line's Shanghai manager, Oscar Steen, was able to stay in contact with the ships. When a CAF plane mistakenly dropped bombs near the civilian *Hoover,* the captains of all commercial shipping refused to come any further up the Whangpoo.

A trickle of British residents began to arrive at the Shanghai Club on the Bund to register their wives and children for evacuation to Hong Kong on the P&O liner *Rajputana*. Sunday morning that trickle would become a flood. The American Consulate called on all American citizens north of Soochow Creek to evacuate the area. Randall Gould, still plane- and fire-spotting from the roof of Broadway Mansions on the northern bank of the creek finally had to come down from his watchtower when the building, home to many American and other Shanghailander families, was formally evacuated.

Dogfights continued into the early evening between Chinese and Japanese planes. Around 5.15 p.m., just three-quarters of an hour after the fateful bombs on the Settlement, a squadron of Chinese planes wrestled with Japanese fighters over the far reaches of the French Concession to the west of the city. After some engagement, which fascinated Chinese and Shanghailanders who stood and watched despite the danger, the faster Chinese planes sped off away from the city. Seven Chinese spectators were killed on the streets of Frenchtown by falling shrapnel. Chinese bombers made another run at the *Idzumo*, but managed only to destroy a sampan and the Chinese family it belonged to. Another bomb hit and destroyed the Jukong Wharf. The wharves and godowns along the Pootung shoreline were major targets. The recently built and very modern wharf of the Japanese steamship company N.Y.K. was partially destroyed by Chinese bombs, which also took ten Chinese lives.

The French Concession authorities feared that a plane would spiral out of control and land on their streets. The Japanese claimed to have brought down one Chinese plane that had tried to bomb Japanese positions in Hongkew; it had crashed into the Japanese cemetery in north-eastern Shanghai. The *Conseil Municipal* that administered the French Concession announced a no-fly zone for either Chinese or Japanese planes over what they declared was French territory. Overnight French anti-aircraft batteries were mobilised to enforce the no-fly zone. Despite protests from both the Chinese and Japanese air forces, the zone was ultimately respected.

In the northern districts of Shanghai, war raged on with ten thousand Japanese troops fighting thirty thousand defending Chinese soldiers. At 6.30 p.m. a lone Japanese seaplane flew up the Whangpoo from Woosung and circled the city against the twilight. A few minutes later a single CAF plane flew over the Settlement from Lunghwa in the west, heading towards the Whangpoo and the circling Japanese aircraft. As the Chinese plane approached the river, the *Idzumo's* deafening anti-aircraft guns cracked the sky. Both planes retreated.

Artillery and field gun fire wracked Chapei throughout the night and extended into the neighbouring Chinese district of Paoshan, which was on fire. The Chinese command relocated from the North Railway Station to a hastily arranged bombproof shelter nearby. The penultimate news of the day was that two additional Japanese divisions were nearing the city and would enter northern Shanghai the following morning. The final news was a press release from the Shanghai Municipal Police stating that the bombs at the Cathay Hotel had killed five hundred and eighty-two civilians. The French *gendarmes* announced that the bombs at the Great World had killed four hundred and fifty people with a further seven hundred and fifty wounded. Both these initial estimates were to be woefully short of the tragic final count and would grow by the day as more bodies were recovered and others died. Herr Boss, the manager of the Palace Hotel, had finally managed to clamber through every room of the establishment. The death toll was sixty members of staff and fifty guests.

Bud Ekins and John Morris were back out covering the fighting in Chapei and Kiangwan during the night of 14 August, as they had done for the previous two days. It was a dangerous beat – not solely due to the threat of bombs and snipers. Their *United Press* colleague John Goodbody had been cornered in Hongkew by a group of angry Japanese soldiers and badly beaten. Ekins headed up to the North Railway Station shortly after 8 p.m., which was still in Chinese hands but under heavy shelling from Japanese forces. He had taken to wearing a surplus army tin helmet given the prodigious amount of sniping from Chinese soldiers and the resultant bursts of random gunfire the Japanese offered in return. It was a wise investment – a bullet pinged off his helmet leaving a severe dent.

Ekins noted that China was giving almost as good as it was getting – Chinese artillery destroyed the Japanese-owned Kung Dah Cotton Mills on Yangtz-epoo's Ping Liang Road and scored several direct hits on Hongkew's Little Tokyo, including the Japanese Girl's High School. They started fires in the densely packed, mostly Japanese-occupied houses. Ninety patients had to be evacuated from the American-run St. Luke's Hospital in Hongkew, on the corner of Boone and Seward Roads. The patients were ferried across Soochow Creek to a makeshift clinic at St. John's University in the far west of the city by Jessfield Park.

Arc lights were erected by Tonkinese Indo-Chinese French troops around the Great World. Elsewhere in the Concession the *Conseil Municipal* ordered a total blackout. Frenchtown, usually lit up with the floodlights of the Canidrome dog racing track and a couple of hundred neon lights and flashing store fronts along the Avenue Joffre, went completely dark. The French authorities, with help from the Chinese and International Red Cross as well as several troops of the Chinese Boy Scouts who had also volunteered, worked hard. One reporter noted that, by evening, the dead from the Great World explosions had been stacked seven feet deep on the pavement outside. Trucks were hastily converted for use as ambulances and hearses. There were shell craters twenty feet deep in Thibet Road and the bombs had fractured sewer and water mains, which made the rescue conditions atrocious. The Japanese ordered a blackout in all the territory they now controlled north of Soochow Creek.

Every hospital in the Settlement was full to bursting with wounded civilians. The city's morgues were full to overcrowding. Many were identified, particularly the foreigners, but many, many Chinese, and a few Shanghailanders, remained unidentified and unclaimed. Others had simply vanished. News of more dead Shanghailanders filtered out – a Russian woman called Mrs Belinsky; Rose Nashtevsky, a Russian telephonist; Mr E.S. Rim, an employee of the Municipal Council; Mr U.F. Lind, a Swedish dredge worker and 'Dodo Dynamite', an American barmaid whose real name was the decidedly less exciting Mrs Scott. The lists of the Chinese dead were so long they were reported simply as totals rather than as individuals.

Admiral Harry Yarnell had made swift progress in the ten thousand ton *Augusta* down the northern coast of China from Tsingtao and was in Shanghai by 8.40 p.m. Yarnell moored three miles upriver from the Settlement on the Whangpoo and prepared to meet with America's Ambassador to China Nelson T. Johnson, who was driving towards the city from Nanking. Yarnell remained aboard and established a direct line of communication with America's Consul General in Shanghai, an old China hand called Clarence Gauss who had first been posted to Shanghai in 1912. Aboard the *Augusta*, nine hundred Marines were on alert and ready to go ashore when commanded. Yarnell had ordered other ships in the Asiatic Fleet to proceed to Shanghai. When they arrived, and with the Fourth Marines already ashore, America would have three thousand troops with which to defend the Settlement if the Japanese moved to occupy the area. Additional French and British troops were disembarked from their respective ships on the Whangpoo, loaded into army trucks and dispersed to take up positions around the Settlement.

Weather conditions deteriorated once more as night fell. The city was lashed with heavy rain and winds which had the benefit at least of reducing the risk of further Japanese advancement into Chapei and Paoshan. During the day, a division of the SVC's Russian Company had found itself isolated in its training camp and behind

Japanese lines out at Alcock Road in the far eastern Yangtzepoo district. The men were ordered to evacuate the camp and begin a long five-day trek across the north of Shanghai through the nearby countryside to eventually re-enter the city in the far west of the Settlement. They were periodically caught in the crossfire between skirmishing Chinese and Japanese on their forced march and lost three men to sniper fire.

The American patrol vessel *Sacramento* arrived and moored up on the Whangpoo, just off the French Concession, with the express aim of guarding the Shanghai Power Company plant. Following the explosions at the Asiatic Petroleum Company facility, further explosions had been reported at both the American Socony-Vacuum Oil terminal and the Texaco terminal. The crew of the *Sacramento* spread a giant Stars and Stripes flag on the deck of the ship to ensure that there would be no mistaking the vessel for a combatant.

A few hours after the *Augusta's* arrival, the Royal Navy's *HMS Cumberland* reached Shanghai, the flagship of Britain's China Squadron under the command of Vice-Admiral Sir Charles Little, who arrived himself shortly afterwards on *HMS Falmouth*. Two hundred British Marines were landed to bolster the nine hundred and fifty soldiers already in the Settlement. Another Royal Navy vessel, *HMS Duncan*, was steaming from Hong Kong with a battalion of the Royal Welsh Fusiliers and a contingent of the Ulster Rifles aboard – they were due to arrive on the 18th and quarters were being prepared for them. A squadron of newly arrived Italian Marines commandeered a school near the Quai de France.

The British organised a convoy of trucks to go down into Yangtzepoo and salvage the belongings of British residents left behind in the rush to evacuate. The British Consulate on the Bund, shaken badly by a falling bomb, had been forced to evacuate its building for the Metropole Hotel further into the Settlement. The diplomats awaited instructions from London as to whether to organise the wholesale evacuation of Shanghai's eight thousand British residents. Admiral Little, who had witnessed the dreadful massacre of the Greeks at Smyrna fifteen years previously, advised a full evacuation; the British Embassy in Nanking was inclined to agree. However, calmer voices from the Shanghai Municipal Council dissuaded London of a full and immediate evacuation. Others felt differently – two hundred and fifty Scandinavian women and children did evacuate to Hong Kong. The British formally warned the Nanking government about the bombs that had fallen from Chinese planes close to *HMS Cumberland*. They were willing to accept it had been a mistake, but Nanking was cautioned to take greater care after the disastrous events of the day.

Claire Lee Chennault had flown down the Yangtze Valley from Nanking to Shanghai that Saturday morning, dodging ominous black rain clouds all the way. His flight had been severely delayed because of the bad weather. The pilot followed the Whangpoo River's outline to land at the Lunghwa Aerodrome to the west of the Settlement. As his plane came in to land, Chennault could see the rolling farmlands of Pootung to the east and the imposing European-style Bund to the west. He also saw Chinese bombers making an attack run at a vessel on the river and the anti-aircraft guns blazing back from the decks of the battleship. Chennault was horrified to see that the vessel under attack was the British cruiser *Cumberland* with a huge Union Jack painted on its afterdeck. Chennault discovered upon landing just how disastrously wrong the day had gone.

The American Consulate was also waiting for a decision on full-scale evacuation from Washington – it would be a massive task and could mean moving up to four thousand people. The French cruiser *Lamotte Picquet* arrived and moored opposite the French Concession on the Pootung side, disgorging fifty French soldiers who marched to their barracks in the Concession; along the Quai de France opposite were moored a French cruiser, a destroyer and two sloops awaiting orders to evacuate French citizens from Shanghai. The German and Dutch Consulates also warned their nationals to be ready for possible full-scale evacuation. Captain Benson of the Royal Navy battle cruiser *HMS Danae* appealed to Admiral Hasegawa to move the *Idzumo* away from the Settlement to prevent any repeat of the day's tragedies. Hasegawa refused. Eleanor B. Roosevelt wrote to Premier Prince Fumimaro Konoye, asking him to withdraw his battleship from central Shanghai to minimise the risk of Chinese air raids. Konoye never replied.

Harry Yarnell was still aboard the *Augusta*. He ordered the cruiser's anti-aircraft guns to be made ready and to fire on any aircraft that seemed likely to repeat the bomb attacks on the Settlement. By now the *Augusta* had moved downriver. Crowds watched as it moored up on the Whangpoo and pointed its guns at the Japanese Consulate. The *Augusta* and the *Sacramento* had been joined by the Yangtze River patrol boat *Tutuila* and the oil tanker *Ramapo*. The *Peary*, a destroyer, was due to arrive at Shanghai in the early hours of the morning. Discussions were in place between Yarnell and Consul General Gauss on how best to move American citizens in Shanghai to Manila, should Washington order an evacuation.

Both the Cathay and the Palace Hotel evacuated and relocated all their remaining guests to other accommodation that evening. Shortly before doing so, a mob of frightened Japanese citizens clustered around the lobby of the Cathay demanding shelter, jostling with the Shanghai Municipal Police officers who were guarding the doors. Eventually, these refugees, and other homeless Chinese, were taken to Yangtzepoo Field in the far east of the Settlement where the Japanese were building an aerodrome and had several large hangars that had escaped destruction.

From Nanking, Chiang Kai-shek announced that he was launching a full enquiry into what had gone wrong, how Chinese planes had dropped Chinese bombs on Chinese people in a Chinese city. To the numerous rumours swirling around the bombings, Chiang added another: Japanese bullets had hit the bomb racks of the planes, releasing the projectiles prematurely. Madame Chiang took to the radio airwaves, in her impeccable English courtesy of her time at Wellesley College, and made the same claim.

Eleanor B. Roosevelt and her son Quentin had left the bombed out Cathay that afternoon unscathed and made their way immediately to the American Consulate where Consul General Gauss was in his office communicating with the American Embassy in Nanking, the State Department in Washington and Admiral Yarnell upriver on the *Augusta*. Gauss had been relieved to see that the Roosevelts were alive and well as Colonel Theodore Roosevelt Jr., Eleanor's husband, has been threatening to fly out to Shanghai personally to find them. He immediately cabled the news to the President that his cousins were safe. Eleanor telegraphed Madame Chiang in Nanking that, '. . . as a sincere friend', she hoped

Madame and her husband would do all they could to avoid a repeat of the attacks. Later, when the sequence of events became clearer, she would follow up her first telegraph to Madame Chiang and wire,

> None deplore more than we the terrible, tragic, accidental dropping of bombs from two damaged airplanes. I personally witnessed casualties and destruction among these people beyond realisation.

Madame Chiang replied to Eleanor,

> The Generalissimo had ordered specifically that no bombs be dropped south of Soochow Creek. Our officers reported that anti-air gunnery wounded both pilots, and killed one on-board machine gunner, while also damaging the bomb racks, causing the bombs to be loosed. It is incredible that the belief exists that China deliberately bombed the International Settlement.

The American Consulate was a crowded place that evening. As well as the Roosevelts and numerous callers seeking news of relatives, colleagues and friends, the remainder of the deceased Dr Robert Reischauer's party had been moved, with their luggage, from the Palace Hotel to the consulate. They were in a sombre mood having heard news of the death of their friend and leader. Eventually, it was arranged for them to be relocated to a French Concession hotel.

That night the Japanese struck back, bombing the Hungjao Aerodrome to the west of the city. The Chinese responded by scuttling additional ships to reinforce the barrier across the Whangpoo, while the evacuation of Kiangwan and Chapei continued. The numbers funnelling across the Garden Bridge onto the Bund and into the Settlement was swelled by a mass evacuation of Wayside. The Wayside District was located between Hongkew and Yangtzepoo, adjacent to the mostly Japanese-owned wharves on the river and the major target that was the Shanghai Water Works.

Associated Press reported that the city '. . . was stilled, out of horror over Saturday's tragedy'. That night, usually the busiest of the week for the city's countless bars, nightclubs, cabarets and restaurants, was eerily quiet apart from patrolling soldiers and the muted, cloth-shoe tread of the countless refugees who had crossed Soochow Creek looking for a doorway, an alleyway or some quiet corner to lie down in. The *New Yorker's* Mickey Hahn was due to dine that evening with Chinese friends. Her host arrived, as did she, but he apologised that they would be dining alone. He explained the reduced party with nonchalance, saying, 'So sorry the other guests will not be here. They were all badly wounded in Nanking Road.' Dining in the restaurant at the top of the Park Hotel on the Bubbling Well Road, opposite the racecourse, Hahn saw Chapei burning. Only the Metropole Cinema went ahead with its new weekly movie programme and, without perhaps recognising the incongruousness of their choice, announced that they would be screening the Edward G. Robinson movie, *Thunder in the City*.

The Day After
Sunday, 15 August, 1937

On Sunday morning, Shanghai awoke to gusty winds and low hanging clouds; the faint glow of fires could be seen in the Settlement and Frenchtown, across to the north in Chapei, Paoshan and Kiangwan, as well as to the east across the vast Pootung marshlands, wharves and godowns on the right bank of the Whangpoo.

The typhoon hadn't dissipated as fast as hoped for. Visibility was extremely low and the city prayed this would stop any repeat bombing runs from the air. Typhoon warning flags were re-hoisted across the city. Machinegun fire from the Chapei frontline could be heard and occasionally shells were fired from the *Idzumo* into the Chinese quarters. There had been periodic shelling of northern Shanghai since 2.30 a.m. The rain did little to dampen the fires in eastern

Chapei, which were largely left untreated; concern mounted that fires could spread from wooden building to wooden building and reach still densely populated Hongkew. The city's gas supplies were cut off by order of the Municipal Council to prevent conflagration if a mains pipe were to be hit by the constant shelling. Shortages were a concern and food prices had shot up by 40 per cent overnight.

Of more immediate concern was the need to clear the dead from the devastated portions of the Settlement and Frenchtown. It was to be a long and gruesome job, hampered by continual fighting and shelling to the north and the threat of more accidental bomb drops to the south, as well as petrol and manpower shortages. Some bodies, predominantly Chinese, were to remain uncollected for several more days, left to decompose on the streets.

The New York Times correspondent Hallet Abend arrived in the city from Nanking four days after the blasts. He visited the Cathay and walked from the Bund up Nanking Road as far as the Sincere and Wing-on Department Stores. The typhoon had completely passed by then and the temperatures had soared back to the mid-nineties with high humidity. Abend claimed the street still smelt like a 'charnel house' and that he saw human tissue and streaks of blood on billboards and buildings that were out of reach of the emergency crews.

On Sunday, further foreign troops poured into the city from arriving naval craft. The British and Americans had approximately two and a half thousand troops each to defend the Settlement, bolstered by seven hundred and fifty Italian Marines. In the French Concession the total troop deployment had reached four thousand, half of whom were Annamese troops from Indo-China.

Claire Lee Chennault was back in Nanking on the roof of the Nanking Metropole Hotel. Late Saturday evening, Japanese wireless stations had announced that Nanking would be bombed that same day. He was joined by several foreign newspapermen.

Chinese fighters patrolled the skies over the capital. After lunch, the city's air raid siren system started to wail. The Imperial Japanese Air Force were confident and arrogant, expecting no effective defence by the CAF. Chennault had ordered the local airfield cleared and consequently, no planes on the ground were destroyed. After the disaster of the day before, the CAF made up somewhat for its errors by spectacularly fighting back and downing eight Japanese aircraft over the capital. In a further success for the CAF, they vigorously defended an attack on the Central Aviation School at Hangchow. Twelve Japanese Navy torpedo bombers took off from the aircraft carrier *Kaga* on the Whangpoo, flying towards Hangchow with the obvious intention of crippling the CAF's main base. The CAF downed eleven of the Japanese bombers and crippled the twelfth.

The Hongkew and Yangtzepoo districts were now without either functioning utilities, Municipal Police, foreign troops or SVC companies. This meant that over three thousand acres of the Settlement's total five and a half thousand acres were effectively under Japanese Army control. The situation alarmed the Municipal Council, who were more than aware that the Settlement's waterworks, gas and electric power stations were now unreachable behind Japanese lines. Rumours whirled that the Japanese were going to poison the city's water supply. Also cut off north of Soochow Creek were many of the Settlement's major wharves and godowns, as well as the Ward Road Gaol, the world's largest prison in 1937. Most of these facilities were being guarded by stranded Sikh watchmen and some Volunteers Corps members. Manpower could be resupplied from the river, but whoever was tasked with the job would be virtual prisoners of the Japanese Army, stranded east of Hongkew.

The French Concession was intact, with no Japanese troop presence on its soil. In addition to their no-fly zone, the French placed Annamese guards outside the various Catholic institutions in Siccawei, just beyond the western borders of Frenchtown, including the observatory, which supplied all the city's crucial meteorological information. Both the International Settlement and Frenchtown were in effective lockdown.

Bud Ekins was back in northern Shanghai, which was still being pounded by Japanese artillery. Early that morning, he wrote,

> The whole sky was aglow from the flames and presented a terrible picture as sulphurous clouds, driven by the wind plowed into the billowing smoke. There were occasional deep, rumbling explosions as chemicals in factories were reached by the flames.

In the space of one night, Shanghai had gone from the legendary 'Paris of the East' to become a dark, frightened city of refugees. The dispossessed continued to swarm into the ten square miles of the International Settlement and the French Concession. Within a few weeks the foreign-controlled portions of Shanghai saw their population rise from one and a half to over four million – most were living in the hundred and seventy-five hastily established refugee camps across the city. Rhodes Farmer, walking the streets examining the conditions the refugees had to endure, described the cityscape, 'For endless miles the city's sidewalks became the bedroom of a million refugees.' Many moved on, the wealthier and more able towards Soochow, Hangchow and Nanking; the poorer and less able walked past the sunken barricades on the river and found ferries willing to head north up the Yangtze. In a few days three hundred and fifty thousand refugees left the city on these horrendously overcrowded ships.

Refugees leaving Shanghai from the Quai de France

*

An accurate count of the dead and injured from Bloody Saturday is impossible to arrive at. Early estimates were as high as five thousand, later estimates put the total at between seven hundred Shanghailanders and as many as three thousand Chinese dead. J.B. Powell, a highly reputable journalist and editor of the *China Weekly Review*, gave the dead at two thousand and the wounded at (at least) two and a half thousand – predominantly Chinese. A report compiled by the French Concession police put the figure at one hundred and fifty dead on Nanking Road and six hundred and seventy-five outside the Great World. But so many died in the side streets, on hospital gurneys and in their homes that a truly accurate number is impossible. Even if the lowest estimates are to be accepted, Shanghai was still the worst ever scene of civilian casualties from aerial bombing to that date.

On Saturday 14 August 1937, Shanghai had awoken to bad weather but a peaceful day. That had been shattered at precisely 4.27 p.m. The press were quick to dub the day 'Bloody' or 'Black Saturday'. Things had changed for Shanghai forever, from Bloody Saturday, as Bud Ekins wrote, '. . . the city's very streets became battlegrounds'. Vanya Oakes added, 'August 1937, saw the peace of the world annihilated, from the Far East.'

APPENDIX OF LANDMARKS

Since the Second World War, most of Shanghai's streets have been renamed. A list of the streets and their current names is given below. Throughout this book I have used the Wade-Giles romanisations of Chinese provinces, districts, rivers, creeks, towns and cities. Thesewould have been in common use in 1937. I list the current pinyin romanisations below. Most of the buildings mentioned are now used for other purposes and I have listed these below too.

Roads:

Alcock Road	Anguo Road
Amherst Avenue	Xinhua Road
Boone Road	Tanggu Road
Brenan Road	Changning Road
Bubbling Well Road	Nanjing West Road

The Bund	Zhongshan No.1 Road
Columbia Road	Panyu Road
Connaught Road	Kanding Road
Dixwell Road	Liyang Road
Avenue Edward VII	Yanan Road
Foochow Road	Fuzhou Road
French Bund *see Quai de France*	
Great Western Road	Yanan Road West
Jinkee Road	Dianchi Road
Avenue Joffre	Huaihai Road
Jukong Road	Zhongxing Road
Kiukiang Road	Jiujiang Road
Markham Road	Huai'an Road
Nanking Road	Nanjing Road East
Pakhoi Road	Beihai Road
Ping Liang Road	Pingliang Road
Quai de France	Zhongshan No.2 Road East
Range Road	Wujin Road
Scott Road	Shanyang Road/ Shande Road
Seward Road	Changzi East Road
Shantung Road	Shandong Middle Road
Route Stanislas Chevalier	Jianguo Road
Szechuen Road North	Sichuan Road North
Thibet Road	Xizhang Road

Yu Yuen Road	Yuyuan Road
Yuan Ming Yuan Road	Yuanmingyuan Road

Places:

American Club	Foochow Road, former US Court for China at Shanghai building (now empty)
Astor House Hotel	Pujiang Hotel, 15 Huangpu Road
Avenue Joffre Fire Station	Huaihai Road Fire Station
Broadway Mansions	20 Suzhou North Road
Cathay Cinema	870 Huaihai Middle Road
Cathay Hotel	Peace Hotel, 20 Nanjing East Road
Cathedral Boy's School/ Shanghai Cathedral	219 Jiujiang Road
Central Fire Station	Guangdong Road
Civic Centre	Jiangwan Stadium
Country Hospital	Huadong Hospital, 221 Yanan West Road
Customs House	13 Zhongshan East Road
French Police HQ	Jianguo East Road
Great World	Corner of Yanan Road and Xizhang Road

Hongkew Park	Lu Xun Park, 146 Jiangwan East Road
Jessfield Park	Zhongshan Park
St. John's University	1575 Wanhangdu Road
Lester Chinese Hospital	Renji Hospital, 145 Shandong Middle Road
St. Luke's Hospital	Shanghai Chest Hospital, 241 Huaihai West Road
Metropole Cinema	500 Xizhang Middle Road
Metropole Hotel	180 Jiangxi Middle Road
Missions Building	169 Yuanmingyuan Road
National Bank of China	Bank of China, 23 Zhongshan East Road
North-China Daily News Building	AIA Insurance, 17 Zhongshan East Road
North Railway Station	Shanghai Railway Museum, 200 Tianmu East Road
Palace Hotel	Swatch Art Peace Hotel, 23 Nanjing East Road
Park Hotel	170 Nanjing West Road
Polytechnic Public School	Shanghai Gezhi High School, 66 Guangxi North Road

Poste Mallet	Yanan East Road
Race Club	Shanghai Art Museum, 1515 Nanjing West Rd
Shanghai Racecourse	People's Park
Shanghai Club	Ritz Carlton Hotel, 2 Zhongshan East Road
Sincere Department Store	479 Nanjing East Road
Union Church	107 Suzhou South Road

Districts:

Chapei	Zhabei
Hongkew	Hongkou
Hungjao	Hongqiao
Kiangwan	Jiangwen
Lunghwa	Longhua
Paoshan	Baoshan
Pootung	Pudong
Siccawei	Xujiahui
Soochow Creek	Suzhou Creek
Wayside	Tilanqiao
Whangpoo River	Huangpu River
Woosung	Wusong
Yangtzepoo	Yangshupu

Cities and Provinces:

Amoy	Xiamen
Canton	Guangzhou
Hangchow	Hangzhou
Kiangsu	Jiangsu
Kiangyin	Jiangyin
Nanking	Nanjing
Peking	Beijing
Tientsin	Tianjin
Tsingtao	Qingdao

Jehol   No longer exists as a separate province in China. In 1955, Jehol was divided between Inner Mongolian and the provinces of Hebei and Liaoning.

NOTES

P2 'the bomber will always get through' From Baldwin's speech to Parliament 'A Fear for the Future', 9th November, 1932.

P6 'not ready for war' Claire Lee Chennault & Robert Hotz, *Way of a Fighter*, (New York: GP Puttnam's & Sons, 1949), p.74.

P10 'silent as nighthawks on straw sandals' Rhodes Farmer, *Shanghai Harvest: A Diary of Three Years in the China War*, (London: Museum Press, 1945), p.49-50.

P19 'concrete measures' reported in many newspapers including 'Japanese Cabinet Decides Concrete Measures Needed', *The Daily Messenger*, 14th August, 1937.

P23 'silhouettes loom out of the darkness' Vanya Oakes, *White Man's Folly*, (Boston: Houghton Mifflin, 1943), p.160.

P28 'little squabbles' see Paul French, *Carl Crow – A Tough*

Old China Hand: The Life, Times, and Adventures of an American in Shanghai, (Hong Kong: Hong Kong University Press, 2006), p.162.

P32 'an impenetrable wall' Farmer, *Shanghai Harvest*, p.45.

P33 'slipped in blood' Farmer, *Shanghai Harvest*, p.48.

P37 'dead centre in Asia's first blitz' Farmer, *Shanghai Harvest*, p.46.

P39 'as silent as a morgue.' Farmer, *Shanghai Harvest*, p.46.

P41 'It seemed as if a giant mower', Percy Finch, *Shanghai and Beyond*, (New York: Charles Scribner's & Sons, 1953), p.255.

P43 'with his arms outstretched' Farmer, *Shanghai Harvest*, p.46.

P43 'Flames from blazing cars' ibid.

P43 'like a rag doll', see Eric Niderost, 'Wartime Shanghai: A Tycoon triumphs Over the Emperor', *World War II Magazine*, September 2006.

P45 'sticky sweet stench' Farmer, *Shanghai Harvest*, p.46.

P46 'the street lined with bleeding bodies', 'Americans in Shanghai Find Adventure in War', *The Waco News-Tribune,* 17th August, 1937.

P47 'I saw a white woman', John R. Morris, 'Blood Flows in Shanghai's Torn Streets', *The Des Moines Register*, 15th August, 1937.

P47 'I could see at least fifty', ibid

P51 'vomited into the gutter' Farmer, *Shanghai Harvest*, p.47.

P51 'Any of you lose this?' Farmer, *Shanghai Harvest*, p.48.

P54 'On the first floor were gaming tables', Josef von
   Sternberg, *Fun in a Chinese Laundry*, (New York:
   Macmillan, 1965).

P58 'windows for blocks around', 'Air Bombing's Horror
   Told by Ex-Boro Man', *The Brooklyn Daily Eagle*, 15th
   August, 1937.

P58 'looked mummified', ibid.

P58 'crushed like egg shells' syndicated in many newspapers
   including, M.C. Ford, 'Autos Crushed Like Eggs', The
   Akron Beacon Journal, 14th August, 1937.

P60 'Look for those who are breathing' Oakes, *White Man's
   Folly*, p.167.

P60 'A call came through' R. Somers quoted in Harriet Sergeant, *Shanghai*, (London: John Murray, 1991), p.300.

P61 'Facing that slaughter house' ibid.

P62 'crowds', Slobodchikoff quoted in Sergeant, *Shanghai*,
   p.300.

P63 'The bastards have dropped it' Stewart quoted in
   Sergeant, *Shanghai*, p.300.

P64 'a little shrapnel' Emily Hahn, *China To Me*,
   (Philadelphia: The Blakiston Company, 1944), p.47.

P68 'The Japanese Navy' reported in many newspapers
   including, H.R. Ekins & John R. Morris, 'Three
   Americans, 1,000 Chinese Killed', *Binghamton Press*,
   14th August, 1937.

P72 'It was pitch dark on one side' Farmer, *Shanghai
   Harvest*, p.49.

P73 'Against the walls' Oakes, *White Man's Folly*, p.167.

P85 'as a sincere friend' reported in many newspapers including, 'Bombing of Settlement', *The Guardian*, 16th August, 1937.

P86 'None deplore more than we' ibid.

P86 'The Generalissimo had ordered' ibid.

P87 'was stilled' 'Air War Rocks Shanghai', *Arizona Republic*, 15th August, 1937.

P87 'So sorry' Hahn, *China To Me*, p.46.

P90 'charnel house' Hallett Abend, *My Life in China: 1926-1941*, (New York: Harcourt, Brace & Company, 1943), p. 254.

P93 'The whole sky was aglow' H.R. Ekins, 'Thousands Die in Shanghai War Chaos', *Oakland Tribune*, 15th August, 1937.

P93 'For endless miles' Farmer, *Shanghai Harvest*, p.50.

P95 'the city's very streets', H.R. Ekins, 'Thousands Die in Shanghai War Chaos', *Oakland Tribune*, 15th August, 1937.

P95 'August 1937', Oakes, *White Man's Folly*, p.158.

PHOTOGRAPHS

All images are from the author's personal collection except where indicated below:

P21 Firemen – Virtual Shanghai

P26 *The Age* – The Age Melbourne, 16 August, 1937

P40 Site of the bombing – photograph by and courtesy of Peter Kengelbacher

P40 Bombed Palace and Cathay Hotel – photograph by and courtesy of Peter Kengelbacher

P56 Bomb crater near Great World – Virtual Shanghai

P65 *Newcastle News* – The Newcastle News-Journal (Wyoming), 14 August, 1937

P70 Refugees leaving via Garden bridge – Randall Gould

P94 Quai de France – Virtual Shanghai

ACKNOWLEDGEMENTS

My thanks to Con Slobodchikoff for confirming details about the extraordinary life and career of his father Nicolai Alexandrovich Slobodchikoff, as well as Jo Lusby, Patrizia van Daalen, Imogen Liu and Lena Petzke at Penguin China. I'd like to thank Anne Witchard for her comments on the manuscript in progress, Christian Henriot and the Virtual Shanghai Project (www.virtualshanghai.net/) for help with images and Douglas Clark for suggestions of newspaper sources. I am also grateful to the staff of the London Library as they were more than helpful during my research for this book.

New York Times
Bestseller

Coming to TV Soon
Over 100 000 copies sold worldwide
12 foreign language editions

....

BBC Radio 4
Book of the Week
Winner of the Edgar Award
2013 (Mystery Writers US)
Best Fact Crime
Nominated for the Macavity
Award 2013 (US)
Best Mystery Non-fiction

Winner of the Australian
Book Industry Awards 2012
International Success of the Year
Winner of the CWA
(Dagger Awards) 2013
Non-fiction

For more information visit: *www.midnightinpeking.com*

Follow the
Mysteries . . .

.... **Also by Paul French:** ....

Midnight in Peking:
The Murder That Haunted the Last Days of Old China

The Badlands: Decadent Playground of Old Peking

Betrayal in Paris: How The Treaty of
Versailles Led to China's Long Revolution

The Old Shanghai A-Z

Through the Looking Glass: China's Foreign
Journalists from Opium Wars to Mao

Carl Crow – A Tough Old China Hand: The Life, Times,
and Adventures of an American in Shanghai

Blog: www.chinarhyming.com
Twitter: @chinarhyming

Instagram: @oldshanghaipaul
Email: paul@chinarhyming.com